You Don't Have to Be Wrong

for Me to Be Right

You Don't Have to Be Wrong for Me to Be Right

Finding Faith Without Fanaticism

BRAD HIRSCHFIELD

THREE RIVERS PRESS • NEW YORK

Reader's Group Guide copyright © 2009 by Three Rivers Press,
an imprint of the Crown Publishing Group,
a division of Random House, Inc.

Published in the United States by Three Rivers Press,
an imprint of the Crown Publishing Group,
a division of Random House, Inc., New York.
www.crownpublishing.com

Three Rivers Press and the Tugboat design are registered
trademarks of Random House, Inc.

Originally published in hardcover in slightly different form in the
United States by Harmony Books, an imprint of the Crown
Publishing Group, a division of Random House, Inc., in 2007.

Grateful acknowledgment is made to the University of California
Press for permission to reprint "The Place Where We Are Right" by
Yehuda Amichai, translated by Stephen Mitchell and Chana Bloch,
from *The Selected Poetry of Yehuda Amichai*, copyright © 1996 by
The Regents of University of California. Reprinted by permission.

Library of Congress Cataloging-in-Publication Data
Hirschfield, Brad.
You don't have to be wrong for me to be right : finding faith
without fanaticism / Brad Hirschfield.—1st ed.
p.   cm.
1. Spirituality.   2. Faith.   3. Religions.   I. Title.
BL624.H53   2007
201'.5—dc22   2007024671

ISBN 978-0-307-38298-6

Printed in the United States of America

10 9 8 7 6 5 4 3 2 1

First Paperback Edition

For Becky,
for everything

Contents

It is precisely the multiplicity of opinions that derive from variegated souls and backgrounds which enriches wisdom and brings about its enlargement. In the end all matters will be properly understood and it will be recognized that it was impossible for the structure of peace to be built without those trends that appeared to be in conflict.

—Rabbi Abraham Isaac Kook

From the place where we are right
flowers will never grow
in the spring.

The place where we are right
is hard and trampled
like a yard.

But doubts and loves
dig up the world
like a mole, a plow.

And a whisper will be heard in the place
where the ruined
house once stood.

—Yehuda Amichai, "The Place Where We Are Right"

You Don't Have to Be Wrong

for Me to Be Right

INTRODUCTION

I FLEW INTO SYRACUSE, NEW YORK, TO GIVE A TALK ON A COOL, windy evening in October of 2000. After we landed, I hailed a cab. I noticed a crucifix mounted on the dashboard and a JESUS LOVES ME sticker on the window.

As he pulled out of the airport, the cabdriver, a middle-aged man with a scraggly beard, checked me out in the rearview mirror. "So," he finally asked in the raspy voice of a heavy smoker, "what do you do?"

I hesitated. Every fiber of my being said, *Lie.* I travel one hundred nights a year for the work I do teaching, speaking, and consulting, and although I love and miss my wife and kids, most of the time I relish the adventure of connecting with all the different types of people I meet on the road. At that moment, however, I did not want to connect with the cabbie. All I wanted to do was sit quietly, get to my hotel, brush my teeth, put on a tie, and go give my lecture.

"I'm a rabbi," I said. I couldn't lie. Not because I'm so pious, but somehow, at that moment, it did not feel like the right thing to do.

"A rabbi!" he replied. "There are so many things I want to ask a rabbi." He studied me. "You believe in the Bible, right?"

"Yes," I said, figuring this was not the time to bring up Old Testament, New Testament . . . those distinctions didn't seem relevant.

"What do you think of Jesus?" he asked.

"If you are asking me if I believe that Jesus is God's only son and the only way we can find salvation, no, that's not what I believe about Jesus. If you're asking if I believe that Jesus is one of humanity's great teachers from whom we all can learn, then yes, I believe in that Jesus."

"But if you think Jesus is so great, shouldn't he be your path to salvation?"

"I can believe that Jesus is a great teacher without believing that he is God's son and the only path to salvation. One truth doesn't negate the other. I can love Jesus in my way. And you can love Jesus in yours. There is room for both of our understandings of Jesus."

"*Whoooah!*" he said. "A rabbi who loves Jesus!" He was watching me so intently in his rearview mirror that he drifted off the road. Chunks of gravel flew up from under the wheels as we veered onto the shoulder and then back onto the highway. I didn't know whether he was impressed or offended. Perhaps he felt I was mocking Christianity. Was the price of my honesty going to be death by car wreck?

Even as I clutched the armrest and prepared myself for whatever was coming next, I empathized with the cabbie. I suspected that he lived a life in which his way was the only way, and it was incomprehensible and not just a little bit maddening that everyone didn't share his particular point of view.

I had been there. In the early 1980s, when I was a teenager, I had been a religious fanatic. I had left my family's upscale North Shore Chicago neighborhood to join a group of settlers in the West Bank city of Hebron. I felt absolutely sure of myself, absolutely sure of the meaning and purpose of my life, absolutely sure that my way was the only way to live.

I led tours for Jews through Hebron, with a Bible in one hand and a gun in the other, pointing out every building with a niche for a mezuzah, the handwritten scroll that marks the door of a Jewish home. I showed them that regardless of maps, this land was ours. The Bible was our deed, because, according to the Book of Genesis, Hebron was the place where Abraham, the first Jew, had bought land for the tomb of Sarah, his wife. It is the place where Genesis says Abraham, Sarah, and their children are buried.

Then something happened that shook me to the core. A group of Jewish settlers was attacked. In running down one of the assailants, three of the settlers fired into a school and killed two Palestinian children.

I was stunned by their deaths. When I sought the advice of one of the settlement leaders, he said, "Yes, this is a problem, but it is not a *fundamental problem.*" That was when I knew something horrible had happened. Staying in Hebron was destroying the very things that had brought us there: the desire to take back power and walk the land our ancestors had. These are good things. But even the best things have limits. A lesson that I learned in Hebron was that the best things can become the most seductive—and deadly.

The deaths of those children cracked me open. I realized that perhaps I didn't have all the answers, and the beliefs that had been driving my life were deeply flawed. I found myself suddenly outside the fold of the settlers' movement, and I felt desolate and not just a little bit lonely.

I tried to stay in Israel after the incident, but it wasn't working for me. The feelings of disillusionment and alienation persisted. So I came home. America, even with all of its materialism (much of which I happen to like) and consumerism, its culture of Coca-Cola and McDonald's, felt more spiritually healthy to me than the Holy Land. Because with all of its problems, this is basically a pluralist, inclusive culture; or at least more of its members aspire to that ideal than do the members of any other society I've experienced. I enrolled in the University of Chicago to study religion while remaining a traditionally observant Jew; I wanted a wider perspective on the forces and beliefs that had run my life. I wanted to explore the forest and not just hug one particular tree.

The U of C provided that for me. I was influenced by Jonathan Z. Smith, who gave all religions a hard time but respected them as well. He moved with ease from Cargo Cults to ancient Israel to medieval Islam to the letters of Paul. I was also influenced by Jon Levinson, a warm engaging man with a wicked, derisive sense of humor. I decided to continue on with my studies, and I enrolled in the doctoral program at the Jewish Theological Seminary in Manhattan. I wanted to go into academia. I had no interest in becoming a rabbi.

I felt that rabbis just persuaded other people to imitate the rabbi, that they scored points by getting you to join their institution, and measured success based on how many people they signed up. While that was different from what was going on in Hebron, it seemed so to me only in degree, not in consciousness. I now know that many rabbis aren't like that, but I still feel that too often success for religious leaders of any faith is about getting their students to look, act, and think more as they do. I aspire to use what I know to help people look more like the person they want to be; to find, to use an overused term, "their best self." I try to offer my teachings as a way to do that, not as an instrument of affiliation.

In graduate school I was interested in exploring religious experience and studying the dawn of the Common Era, the historical period that gave birth to both rabbinic Judaism and Christianity. I focused on that era because I felt that that time had been not unlike this time. Old institutions seemed to be failing, new ones were being born, and the world was increasingly a global community. People were confronted with radical changes in citizenship, identity, and spirituality.

As I was writing my dissertation, I was invited to teach a course on Talmud to first-year rabbinical students. As the course progressed, I realized that I was far more interested in my students than in my own research. Many of my students saw problems of spiritual leadership in the United States, and they were trying to redefine what it meant to be a spiritual leader. They moved and inspired and pushed me to become a rabbi. They were living proof that being a rabbi wasn't just about peddling your point of view. They gave me confidence and opened me up.

When I gave the cabbie my take on Jesus that night in Syracuse, I was speaking to him through the prism of my Hebron experience and how it had changed me. I was trying to help him see that my way was not the only way, and that although each of us was deeply committed to a particular tradition, we could remain open to the wisdom found in other traditions. I wanted him to appreciate that I could love and learn from his tradition, and that we did not need to agree in order to share that love.

I assumed the cabbie's strong reaction had to do with the fact that, as he said, he had found a rabbi who loved Jesus. But it was more than that.

"Rabbi, can I tell you a personal story?" he asked.

"Sure."

The cabbie said that for years and years he had been a drug addict and an alcoholic. He had been in and out of detox programs. He had suffered relapses and broken countless promises to himself and others. He had been unable to hold a job and was often in trouble with the law. He had lived his life that way for as long as he could remember. And then he had been introduced to his church and his pastor, had found Christ, and had become clean and sober. Jesus had saved him.

I've talked to many addicts over the years, and I know what a difference Jesus can make in their lives. In Jesus they find a source of unconditional love—an affirmation of human dignity and infinite worth, no matter what transgressions they have committed, an image of someone who suffered more than they have, no matter how much they have suffered. And in Jesus they find someone who literally came back from the dead, who was reborn.

Jesus had showed the cabbie how he could start over, and evangelical Christianity had been his salvation. But, he told me, he had a problem: his wife of twenty years wanted nothing to do with his religion, church, or pastor. "She doesn't go to church with me, and she doesn't want to go to church with me," he said. "She doesn't believe what I believe. But she never gave up on me, through all the dark times. She stuck with me. And now . . ." his voice broke and he couldn't get out the words. "Plus," he finally added, "my pastor says that if she doesn't get the Message, then maybe she isn't the best partner for me."

I could feel how torn he was. His most important teacher had told him that he had a choice to make. He felt pulled in different directions by the two things that mattered most in his life: his wife and his faith. Nobody had told him that his wife could be completely with him on his journey even if they were never going to be in complete agreement. My teacher in Hebron, for whom any difference was an excuse for disconnection, expressed the same mind-set. Either the cause was perfect and for everybody, or it was flawed and therefore for nobody.

"You can make room for each other," I said to the cabbie. "She can be the right woman for you, and you can be the right man for her. You shouldn't do anything different except make room for her as she is."

"Can I still pray for her?" he asked.

"For her to see the light? To believe what you believe?

I guess so. You probably wouldn't be you if you didn't pray for her. But if your praying starts to make you appreciate her less, then you are praying too much. Your wife doesn't have to be wrong for you to be right. And when it comes to Jesus, you don't have to be wrong for me to be right."

By this point, we had arrived at my hotel. The cabbie remained silent as he pulled into the entrance. I wondered if I had offended him. As soon as we stopped, he rushed to open my door. I wasn't sure what was coming next. He pulled me out of the car, reached out his arms, and embraced me. "Thank you, Rabbi," he said. "You would make a good pastor." I felt honored—it was his highest form of praise.

Given the way religion works all too often today—fueling intolerance, inspiring violence, and treating all those who challenge it as dangerous enemies—no one was more surprised than I that the encounter with the cabbie had ended well. If these kinds of stories usually had happy endings, there would be no need for this book.

We live in a world where religion is killing more people than at any time since the Crusades. According to the U.S. State Department, seventy to eighty percent of the world's conflicts are based on religion. There is confusion about the nature of this violence. Kofi Annan, the former secretary general of the United Nations, had the audacity to say recently that the problem is not with the faiths but with the faithful. That's a dodge.

Each of our faiths has a rich tradition that justifies dumping loving spouses for not worshipping in our church, disrupting the lives of those whose very presence dares to interrupt our redemptive reveries, or even murdering those who we have decided are acting against God, simply for acting in ways we disapprove of.

When faith simplifies things that need to remain complex, instead of giving us strength to live with complexity, when it gives answers where none exist, instead of helping us appreciate the sacredness of living with questions, when it offers certainty when there needs to be doubt, and when it tells us that we have arrived when we should still be searching—then there is a problem with that faith.

Religion captures the very best and very worst of who we are, and to see only the best *or* the worst of religion is a dangerous error. If you see only the good, you become an apologist and take no responsibility for the incredible violence that religion is so capable of unleashing. If you see only the bad in religion, then you miss all the biggest questions, the most profound longings, the deepest fears and greatest aspirations that define us. When faith is working right it can be profound, inspiring, and a great force for positive change in the world, and it can help us lead more giving, productive, and fulfilling lives.

Belief is more complicated than either the believers or the disbelievers among us are usually willing to admit. Too often I hear people referring to God as a delusion and religion as some kind of neurological disorder. All their qualms and suspicions are justified. But if all they see is the ugly face of faith and the danger in spiritual connection, they have become as absolute in

their disbelief as any religious fanatic. They have become fanatics of secularism who are as problematic as the fanatics of faith,
because ultimately it is the fanaticism that kills, not the faith.

It is a hard and painful thing for me to admit that religion
is responsible for much of what's wrong in the world today, because I love religion and I love my faith. But that is the way it is
with things, and people, you love: you love them, faults and all.
Early on in our marriage, my wife, Becky, and I had a fight (I
can't remember about what) that unnerved me enough to do
the unconscionable: call my parents.

My father listened patiently to my rant, and then said, "Remember that you marry people because of certain things and
despite certain things."

I have kept that lesson close to me. In marriage, it's made
me realize that you're going to know how much you love each
other when you realize that there are things about each other you
don't love. And it's that way with everything else in our lives. If
we're not willing to take a good hard look at what we love, we
probably don't really love it enough.

This book recounts my journey from the moment I became a traditionally observant Jew from a nontraditional family,
through my experiences in the settlers' movement and then on-
ward to my life as a teacher, talk-show host, and author. My
journey has taken me from the top of the Reichstag, where I
stood with the president of Germany, to the altar of a Catholic
church just outside the gates of the Auschwitz concentration
camp. I have met with imams in Indianapolis and in Morocco, as
well as creationists and people who believe in killing doctors

who practice abortion. It is a journey that has taken me into a marriage and the raising of three daughters.

My work has been about trying to build bridges between people of different faiths, including no faith at all. I have tried to help people discover that no one is ever one hundred percent right or one hundred percent wrong. I have wanted to nurture our ability to make deep commitments while remaining open to new ideas and new experiences. Ultimately my most important goal has been to help people lead happier and more meaningful lives.

This book is for each of us who feels the continuum of conflict that is a part of all of our lives and seems to loom larger for so many of us every day—from the inner stresses that come with balancing more roles, greater complexity, and the quickening pace of our personal lives to the challenges of sustaining relationships with family, friends, and colleagues in a culture that demands quick responses and is often unforgiving of any failings. We live in a moment of polarized politics, angry rhetoric, and increasing violence, often pushed into the unfair choice between fanatical commitments that make us crazy and openness that is so loose it leaves us lonely.

Conflict is an inevitable part of life, a function of being connected to each other, and, often, an opportunity to grow closer. Perhaps it is too much to promise that we can resolve all of our conflicts, but it's not too much to promise that with the right approach we can at least address them more constructively. The chapters of this book offer such an approach; they include concrete steps that all of us can take to successfully address the continuum of conflict. We are more able than we might imagine to take those steps—and it is beautiful when we do.

I don't know all the answers, but I do know that I've had remarkable teachers and a range of experiences that I want to share. Those experiences include being one of the "crazies," one of the fanatics. After 9/11, I felt that I wanted to explain the religious impulse at its most extreme, to dig into the anatomy of fanaticism, really to probe the destructive tendencies that are part of all religions.

I felt that it was important for me to do this because I knew, at least partially, what had been going on in the minds and hearts and souls of the men who had flown the planes into the Twin Towers. After years of simply avoiding any real examination of that part of my life, it was time to come clean and share my journey into and out of fierce faith, precisely because unlike most people who make that journey, it had left me still in love with what I left behind.

A few days after the 9/11 attack, I stood near the smoldering wreckage at Ground Zero, and I was reminded of Auschwitz. I had the same overwhelming feeling of being present at a place of maximum death. A firefighter came over and told me to move, but I was paralyzed. The only thing that came out of my mouth was, "I'm a rabbi," as if that might make a difference.

I will never know exactly why I blurted it out then, but was reluctant to divulge my identity that night in Syracuse. At Ground Zero I may have been playing the clergy card to score a little extra access to a place I was not yet ready to leave. It could have been that deep down, at really critical moments, I know that's what I am—a rabbi.

"You're a rabbi?" he replied. "I'm Jewish." He was a big guy with a broad chest, and I thought he was going to escort me away; instead he came over and put his face on my shoulder and started to cry. I put my arms around him and we wept together.

Rabbi Shlomo Carlebach, a contemporary Hasidic rebbe and famous Jewish songwriter, once told me what it means to hug. He said that if you want to show someone you love them, you would assume that you should hold their face in your hands and look into their eyes. But if you want to share something even more powerful, you hug the person. In essence you are saying, "I will hold you up. No matter what happens or how bad it gets, I will hold you up."

That is finally what I want this book to be: a guide to our common humanity, and a source of strength and stamina and hope.

CHAPTER ONE

THE MANY FACES

OF FAITH

Finding Faith Without Fanaticism

FAITH CAN BECOME SOMETHING THAT'S NARROW, LIMITING, an either/or that is rigid and unyielding. That is what happened to me in Hebron. I don't think that this faith is true faith. It fact it may be precisely faith's opposite, an extremity of doubt that boomerangs into strident belief.

The essayist Michel de Montaigne wrote, "We are, I know not how, double within ourselves, with the result that we do not believe what we believe and cannot rid ourselves of what we condemn." An even clearer expression of the quixotic and paradoxical quality of faith is this brilliant insight by Reinhold Niebuhr: "Fanatic orthodoxy is never rooted in faith but in doubt; it is when we are not sure that we are doubly sure."

I have been completely taken over by the intoxication of

being "doubly sure." But I have come to know that the true meaning of faith is not to be found in these sureties or in a single absolute, but in *competing* absolutes. Faith is about a loving acceptance of the profound complexity of existence and creation. It is about abiding in mystery, in being unsure, while still being ready to act boldly.

This is how Abraham felt when he looked inside himself and left his home and country to venture forth to find what God said would be "the promised land." Abraham's journey was one of wandering, of not knowing, of discovering. He had nothing except faith—indelible, extraordinary faith.

The women in my family showed me this kind of faith. It is precisely the kind of faith that my great-grandmother had, although she was a devout atheist and the way she lived her life would be a deep disappointment—worse, an unforgivable transgression—to the orthodox Judaism that I practice. So be it. For me, it was my great-grandmother who taught me that faith has many faces.

The middle-class home in which I grew up on the North Shore of Chicago was deeply Jewish, though not conventionally religious. We didn't keep kosher. My father was agnostic, yet he asked my mother not to serve the nonkosher foods of pork and shellfish in the house, and not to mix meat and dairy at the same meal, prohibitions that are part of the laws of kashruth. Synagogue was someplace you went under duress and preferably not more than three or four times a year. Religion per se was not important. But we were deeply identified Jews joyfully engaged in the cultural life of the Jewish community, passionate about Israel, and my parents were also philanthropic. Part of their cultural DNA told them that part of being Jewish meant taking care of other human beings.

Through a strange quirk of faith, my younger brother and I were sent to a Jewish day school. My mother was spooked. My siblings, who are ten and twelve years older than I am, were in high school and the world seemed to be falling apart for people like my parents. Harvard and Princeton—the bastions of achievement and excellence on which they had staked not their lives but the lives of their children—were in the throes of the counterculture of the 1960s: drugs, rebellion, and antiwar demonstrations. Nice Jewish kids were turning on and dropping out. Children who have since become doctors, lawyers, scientists, and scholars were growing their hair long, parading around in torn jeans, smoking grass and worse, and occupying the administrative offices of the very institutions on which their futures hinged. In short, my parents thought, these kids were doing everything in their power to destroy their own lives (not to mention what my parents knew of civilization). That's why my younger brother and I were sent to a Jewish day school—for the values, for stability, for *tradition*!

But my parents were startled when, in the seventh grade, I embraced their decision and became religiously observant. They were even more startled when I chose to go to the Ida Crown Jewish Academy, an orthodox high school in Chicago.

Why did I become an orthodox Jew? It's hard to say. I fell in love, and I can no more tell you exactly why than I can tell you why I fell in love with my wife. In both observant Judaism and my wife, I saw beauty and wisdom. I saw purpose, direction, focus, and meaning. I was euphoric, and I felt swallowed up.

I read omnivorously, trembling with excitement, on the edge of myself. I devoured every book about Judaism that I could find. I read Abraham Joshua Heschel, one of the great philosopher-poets of Jewish life in the twentieth century, and Samson Raphael Hirsch, a nineteenth-century German Jew and leading rabbi who tried to integrate total commitment to Jewish tradition with his desire to live fully as a German. I read the *Jewish Catalogue,* a 1970s guide to making your own Judaism, and *To Be a Jew: A Guide to Jewish Observance,* an orthodox treatise by Rabbi Hayim Havely Donin. I wanted to learn everything that I could about being Jewish. Becoming an observant Jew was an expression of my passion and excitement.

I knew that my family considered itself part of the Conservative movement in Judaism (although they didn't live in a way that would pass muster with a Conservative rabbi). By becoming orthodox I was making a big leap. Orthodox Jews believe that the Bible is a direct gift from God, while Conservatives think it was inspired by God but produced by human beings. Orthodox Jews tend to be *much* stricter and more rigorous in Jewish ritual practice than Conservatives. This kind of devotion—this all-encompassing version of faith—was foreign to the Hirschfield home.

My parents were a bit perplexed by my desire to become ritually observant. But my great-grandmother, Sarah Plotkin, the matriarch of our family, was appalled. Sarah Plotkin lived to . . . ninety-eight? One hundred? We don't know. She was older than her husband, something we only discovered when she died, and lied about her age her whole life.

The Matriarch lived in Palm Springs. She liked it there: good climate, plenty of sun, dry. You didn't have to worry about mildew or shoveling snow. Two of her six kids lived with her. They were unmarried; they had been raised to wait on the queen.

My grandparents also lived in Palm Springs. When we visited them, after going out to dinner, we would go to *bubbe*'s. Even in her nineties, *bubbe* didn't miss a trick. We all thought she was going blind and deaf, but my father used to say that if you dropped a twenty-dollar bill across the room, she could read the serial number going down and hear it hit the floor.

She sat in her special chair, a big Barcalounger with a handle on the side that operated a footrest. A diminutive woman with an iron will, she piled her white hair on top of her head to make herself look taller, and dressed in chartreuse, mauve, and apricot silk robes. She loved jewelry (rings and big gold bracelets) and male singers. She thought Tom Jones was sexy and wasn't afraid to say so into her nineties as Jones pranced around, live from Las Vegas, on her television.

One evening visit to *bubbe* was particularly memorable and important to me.

When I was twelve, I made the decision to wear a yarmulke (*kippah*) full-time. The tradition of wearing a *kippah* in Judaism has mysterious origins. The first time that head covering is connected to piety is in a story in the Talmud (compiled from the second to the sixth centuries C.E.). A mother brings her errant son to a rabbi, who tells her to wrap the boy's head in a *sudra,* the Aramaic word for the head wrapping that rabbis wore. Then all will be well, he assures her.

What does the story mean? The rabbi may have been suggesting that if you dress like a priest or rabbi you will begin to feel like one. There is a connection between what you wear and what you feel, between how you look and who you are.

By the Middle Ages, when wearing a yarmulke was normative for male Jews, it had become a reminder of the immanence of God, keeping you aware of the sacred potential of each moment. But that's not all that it was about for me at twelve. I was declaring who I was to the world. It was an expression of the seriousness of my commitment. I was integrating the physical and spiritual, becoming on the outside who I felt like on the inside. I did it because it felt right. Now wearing a *kippah* has become like putting on my pants in morning. Not putting it on would be like going out into the world in my underwear.

No one else in my family wore a *kippah* except when they went to temple (which, again, was almost never), and I knew it would not go unnoticed by Sarah Plotkin with her hawklike eyes. I bent down to kiss her and she grabbed my hair. "I did not come to America for this foolishness!" she thundered, and tore the *kippah* off my head and threw it on the floor.

I had just made the commitment to become observant. I was excited about my choice, inspired, and perhaps a little bit tentative. But to my *bubbe* the yarmulke was ridiculous: the thundering voice of the Matriarch was calling me an idiot!

I was a deer in the headlights. My whole family, who already thought the *kippah* was weird, witnessed the scene. I was stunned and hurt, but mostly I was paralyzed. Speechless.

I'll never forget my mother, who stood up straight and said to her own grandmother, with a clear sense of the truth and rightness of her words, "No, *bubbe.* You are wrong. You came to America so that he *could* wear the *kippah* if that's what he wants to do."

That was a great moment for me, a monumental moment. I have studied with great rabbis, brilliant teachers, but at this moment my mother taught me more about the meaning of faith than any of them. She taught me the faith that can be built between a parent and child, in every parent who respects the choices of her children even if she does not agree with them. She was helping me be more like me, not a reflection of who she was. She was showing me a willingness to trust and to believe in the goodness and rightness of the person in front of her. That's a very powerful kind of faith.

My *bubbe* was also teaching me a different lesson. I couldn't see it at the time, of course, but I now know that the very thing she ridiculed was what her *own* life had been about—her own form of faith.

My great-grandparents had set off from Minsk to the United States in the 1890s. They did not do this because they were poor. My great-grandmother, an educated woman, came from a family with servants. My great-grandfather, Sam, was a cabinetmaker with a good living. He knew two things: that he wanted Sarah as his wife, and he wanted to go to America. He was successful here and eventually moved his family to Birmingham, Michigan—at the time, a restricted community. He had to buy his way into the area, paying off neighbors to make it acceptable for them to live next to a Jew. He was honored in the book *Men Who Made Michigan,* a dusty copy of which is still in my parents' home.

My great-grandparents betrayed all the rules of what it meant to be Jewish, and in doing so fulfilled a central commandment in the Bible: choose life!

In the Bible, Deuteronomy 30:19 says, "You should choose life in order that you should live." Jews who can't remember much about their Sunday-school education remember this: that it is permitted that you may break almost every law to save a life.

The rabbis in Minsk said to Sarah Plotkin, "Don't go to America, you will stop keeping kosher." And they were right! She did stop keeping kosher. She stopped observing Shabbat. She abandoned Jewish ritual life. But if my great-grandparents had been worried about ritual, they probably would have stayed in Minsk, and I, in all likelihood, would not be here today, having vanished in either the Holocaust or behind the Iron Curtain. Boarding that boat and setting off for a new world, as so many of our ancestors from so many countries did then (and so many people are still doing today), was *living* faith, choosing and committing to a better life. Which is what our traditions should do for each of us: help us imagine a better world and nurture our ability to get there.

What had possessed my great-grandparents as teenagers in Minsk, eight thousand miles from the California oasis of Palm Springs, to think that they could build a better life for themselves and their children and their children's children in a place where they couldn't even speak the language? What set them off on their long journey? It was the same voice deep inside them, intimately close and infinitely far, that said, as it once had to Abraham, "Go to the land that I will show you."

What act of faith could I engage in to match that? Faith is in its expressions, in the way we live. To live your faith is what my *bubbe* had done, and what I was trying to do with my *kippah* in my own way, and what my mother was doing when she let me make my own choices, believing in me and refusing to let my choices become a journey away from the love we shared.

The story of my deciding to become observant and wear a *kippah* is not a story about coming back to "real Judaism." It is the story about my great-grandparents' faith—in themselves, in the future, in the journey. Like Abraham, my great-grandparents walked away from everything they knew.

One of the many facets of true faith is the ability to wrestle with the big issues: What does my life mean? What does the future hold? It is about committing yourself passionately to the choices you make, although all too often that passion and commitment involves denigrating the choices of others. I understand that impulse. I think all of us can understand it. When you give yourself so fully to something, when you stake who you are on it, you had better be right! You feel you have found yourself and the way to live while all around you is the confusion and chaos of the world. And yet that's what life is like! It's messy and imperfect.

There are as many different kinds of faith as there are people. I learned this lesson early in my childhood. I learned the

commandment to honor my mother and father not at the Shabbat table where a nice Jewish boy on Friday night is supposed to
learn it, but at a Chinese restaurant on Randolph Street.

My grandparents ate out six nights of seven. My grandmother couldn't cook. My grandfather would come home and
they would go out. They were friends with maître d's all over
the Magnificent Mile in Chicago. The Pickle Barrel or the Cape
Cod Room at the Drake Hotel—it didn't matter. Sundays, however, were always reserved for Ho Kow, which had the best
spareribs in Chicago.

Every Sunday my parents would drive us to eat Chinese
food with my grandparents. It was a weekly ritual that turned
into something as special and meaningful to me as Shabbat dinner on Friday night. (My father's mother died before I was born,
and my paternal grandfather died when I was two.) To this day,
when I walk by a Chinese restaurant and I smell food I can't
eat and haven't eaten for thirty years, I remember how my parents showed their respect to my grandparents. I don't smell
spareribs; I smell *Honor your father and mother.* After I became orthodox, I realized that a sparerib can be just as much a transmitter of Jewish tradition as matzo balls. This doesn't mean that
today I eat spareribs at Chinese restaurants (or that I want my
kids to eat them). It's not kosher in the way that I understand
kosher. But anyone who presumes that if you eat pork you can't
teach or live Torah is wrong—dead wrong. The same goes for
driving on Shabbat, another prohibition my parents violated
when my grandparents came to our house for Friday-night dinner and my parents drove them home in my mother's Mercury
Marquis station wagon with the wood trim. Thirty minutes

there, thirty minutes back. What energy that took! What respect, what *reverence* that expressed—to get into the car late at night and schlep all the way to 900 North Michigan Avenue, the top of the Magnificent Mile, right across the street from Oak Street Beach, to my grandparents' elegant old apartment building. I learned that honoring one's parents was crucial, important, the way to live.

My orthodox younger brother, who is also one of my best friends, most trusted confidants, and reliable teachers, would probably throw up at what I just said. To connect "honor your mother and father" to spareribs? To "violating" the Sabbath? He'd think I'd lost my mind.

Religious communities across the board have problems making these kinds of unlikely connections in which a seeming contradiction is actually a sacred teaching. We in the West may feel Islam is intolerant of what it considers blasphemous. We can point to the Twin Towers, or to the Danish cartoons of Muhammad that created such uproar around the world. Countless Muslims did exactly what was expected and behaved in a crazy, maniacal, bloodthirsty way. And the cartoonists and the newspapers that published their work trumpeted their own iconic understanding of freedom of expression, even when that understanding was deployed in a purposefully hurtful way. Both sides were saying, "There are no limitations, and we have no obligations except to ourselves." For them, there is only one un-wavering side to their faith—whether that faith is Islam or freedom of speech.

Plenty of Jews have this same issue. We're not training a generation of young men to strap on explosive vests, but we did murder our own prime minister, and some of our rabbis, both in Israel and elsewhere, have decreed that it may be permissible to take the life of any person in a position of power who takes part in dismantling a settlement or trades land for peace. Plenty of Christians are as blind and narrow in their faith as Jews and Muslims. Ask anyone whose family has been terrorized by members of a so-called Christian Identity church because they happen to be black or gay. Or anyone who has been heckled as she entered a women's health clinic by the well-intentioned members of any evangelical community. Maybe you think that's a situation on a much smaller scale, even while admitting the possibility that it may somehow be the same problem. But the problem is the same. You believe that you have unfettered access to the whole truth, and that your knowledge gives you permission to do whatever you believe is necessary in defense of that truth. And if it's *your* kid who has been beaten to death, the scale is not smaller—not by a long shot. If Yitzhak Rabin was your father or husband, the scale is not smaller.

Traditionalists tend to be suspicious of the present, and think the only way to go forward is to go back. Liberals tend to think that tradition is oppressive, so the future will simply be a reiteration of the present. Our best future, however, will be a creative remix of everything we are and have been.

Which brings me back to food. My favorite food when I was growing up (aside from ribs) was shrimp cocktail. My father's rule was that what we couldn't eat at home, he would buy for us when we ate out. I ordered it every time I saw it on a restaurant menu. It was easy to eat and felt like grown-up food. And I could always order it with ketchup instead of cocktail sauce, which was too spicy, and pretend it was the same thing, which made me feel very grown up.

Whenever we ate out, we said a blessing first—my father's wonderful idiosyncratic Judaism. Making a blessing is a Jewish way of celebrating the moment, and we shared a blessing before each meal. But to make things easier, we said the simple blessing over bread: "Blessed are you, O God, ruler of the Universe, who brings bread out of the earth."

One day in the fifth grade, my teacher was going over the various blessings over different food. I raised my hand and innocently asked: "What is the blessing for shrimp?" She promptly threw me out of class and sent me to the principal's office. She was appalled because not only had I confessed to eating shellfish (Leviticus states that Jews may only eat those fish with fins and scales), but I wanted to know how to celebrate that and call attention to it. A blessing over shrimp was a double whammy.

The principal, Harry Kessler, a short man given to loud ties and an even louder voice, had been in vaudeville before he began teaching. He was a great man because he loved his students more than the ideas he was teaching us.

"Why are you here, Brad?" he asked when I showed up at his door.

"We were studying blessings, and I asked for the blessing for shrimp," I replied.

"Now, why would you ask that?" Harry Kessler cried out in his high-pitched voice.

"Whenever we eat, wherever we are, we say a blessing," I

said. "But we use the blessing over bread. When we go out, I love to eat shrimp cocktail. I wanted to know the correct blessing—the blessing for shrimp."

"Where did you learn this practice?" he asked.

"From my father."

Mr. Kessler studied me. "Do you know what the rabbis teach us about the lessons we learn from our parents and grandparents?" he said. "They teach us that those lessons are like learning from Moses on Mount Sinai."

Then he told me to go back to class.

It amazes me to this day that Mr. Kessler wanted to understand who I was before he resorted to doctrine or dogma. Is this the definition of compassion? It could be. It's my definition based on my life experience. Compassion—or empathy in this case; I don't distinguish between the two—is about noticing the person in front of you before the ideology inside of you. And it's about making choices to privilege that person.

There are resources in every spiritual tradition that would encourage us to ask questions before we offer conclusions. When push comes to shove, the conclusions will come. Harry Kessler understood there was plenty of time down the road to tell me about the prohibition against eating shrimp. This sounds easy to do, but when we think we're in the right, boy, is it hard to hold our tongues: we want to jump to that part of the story—fast.

The choice that Principal Kessler made to affirm what was right in *my* experience instead of showing me the error of my ways was so important to me. I have used it as a compass in my own life, my own teaching.

A final story about faith, family, and food. We need to see that everyone who is not just like us is not some kind of restoration project, just waiting for us to "fix" them and turn them into poor imitations of ourselves. Do we really want a world of people who look, think, and act just like we do? That's not spiritual depth or religious growth, but simply narcissism with lots of footnotes.

When I was twelve years old and made my decision to be orthodox, I went to my mother and asked her to purchase separate pots and pans for me because I wanted to keep strictly kosher. I brought this subject up on one of those evenings in my parents' bedroom when we were hanging out and watching TV.

I asked my mother because I knew that it was up to her to make it happen. I joke that my father had four kids and thirteen grandchildren and never changed a diaper. Anything that had to do with the house was strictly my mother's domain.

I can only imagine what my mother felt at that moment. Did she make a conscious effort to open herself? Did she think, *One more ritual, one more observance, and I'm going to snap? I've bent as far as I can bend.*

Although we didn't mix meat and dairy or eat pork or shellfish in the house, what I wanted was far more than that. I needed separate pots and pans for milk and dairy. I needed meat that was ritually slaughtered and prepared. My mother would have to shop in a completely new way, checking the additives in all prepared foods to make sure they didn't violate the prohibitions of kashruth.

Jewish dietary laws go back to Adam and Eve. "Behold, I have given you every seed-bearing plant and fruit to eat," says God to the first couple, who are vegetarians. They are not allowed to eat meat, which is only given to Noah and his sons after the flood. Again, however, limits are set. Noah has to stay away from blood, which is synonymous with life, according to the Bible.

What we are seeing in Genesis is a creative tension—one that runs through the whole tradition—between human power and capacity and a deep reverence for the sacredness of all life. The laws of kashruth, or keeping kosher, are the next iteration of that same tension in the Book of Leviticus. Kosher recognizes that we can make life and take life, but there have to be rules—and the laws of kashruth make me engage with that creative tension and awareness three times a day (more when I snack).

When I told my mother that I wanted to keep kosher, she looked at me long and hard, her twelve-year-old who had found religion. "I will not buy separate pots and pans and silverware for you," she finally said. "What I will do is this—if you will wait until summer when I have more time, I will make the entire house kosher. You don't eat off separate dishes from the rest of us in your own home." It was as simple as that. "But," she continued, "I hope that keeping kosher will not keep you from going out to dinner with us, because that's also part of what it means to be a family."

Without knowing exactly how I would do it, I gave my word that I would continue to go out with them—and after that fateful conversation I dined at some of the world's finest restaurants and ate only salad while my family feasted. Although I love to eat, it was never a problem. People often ask me about the effort it takes to keep kosher and observe the exacting prescriptions of Jewish law. I don't think of it as difficult. I love doing it, and it never feels oppressive. But here's where it gets complicated. It's a choice, but also an obligation. It's a choice about choicelessness.

In that way, being orthodox is a lot like a marriage and a lot like parenting. When we are faithful to spouses or children, is it because we've chosen to be or must be? I chose my wife, but after seventeen years of marriage I can honestly say that infidelity is not an option—and this is not because I'm so holy. I don't feel I have a choice. Having chosen, I have given up my right to choose.

When someone says to me, "Why don't you eat pork?" and I say I can't, that is not because I am incapable of wolfing down a pork chop (I can), or that I believe I would burst into flames if I did (I wouldn't). I know for a fact that even while eating pork and afterward I wouldn't *feel any less Jewish*. I don't eat pork because that is just the way it is—*for me*. That's what is most crucial to remember: what is obvious and obligatory for one of us is not so for all of us, but that does not dilute the potency of our own commitments and faith.

Choice leads to choicelessness, in the best way. It leads to genuine obligation, which is never experienced as coercive when it is truly genuine. That is what my mom felt when I asked her to help me be kosher. This request was a genuine obligation, the love of a mother to her son.

My mother also understood that being who I needed to be was not a rejection of her or of the rest of my family as long as I was staying connected to them. Instead of saying, "You'll be lost to me," she sent me the clear message that she wanted to help me be who I wanted to be, but not at the price of disconnecting with who I had *been*.

My mother found herself a kosher butcher, Shaevitz's, on Devone Avenue in West Rogers Park, then the heart of Chicago's orthodox community—a neighborhood in which she would never have otherwise set foot.

Shaevitz was a rough-looking man with a permanent five-o'clock shadow who somehow made this North Shore lady, who had grown up with a Christmas tree in her home, comfortable in his store. He made my mother feel welcome with all his other customers, most of them orthodox Jewish women in long dresses and covered hair, who must have been at least a little surprised when my mother waltzed into Shaevitz's in her country-club garb, a short tennis skirt and perfume. To them she was an apparition from beyond the Pale.

I grew up in the neighborhood where *Risky Business* and *Ordinary People* were filmed. When my mother went to West Rogers Park to buy the brisket that I loved, she must have felt she was going to Anatevka, the shtetl village where *Fiddler on the Roof* is set. She made that trip while I was wandering around our secular neighborhood in a *kippah* and walking, like the eponymous character in the Philip Roth story "Eli, the Fanatic," three miles each way to synagogue on Shabbat.

My mother did not know any orthodox Jews—until, that is, she met her twelve-year-old son in his *kippah* who wanted to keep kosher. She could easily have run screaming from the house when I told her I wanted my own pots and pans and plates and silverware.

Faith in me, faith in God—for my mom, those ideas were largely interchangeable. My *bubbe's* denial of God was also an expression of faith. Her faith in herself and her husband and the future they would have together in a distant land was part of the deepest rhythms of their tradition—to go and find a better life for themselves and their family.

My mother expressed her faith by allowing me to make choices. She was comfortable enough with who she was to help me be who I wanted to become. She believed in me. She trusted me, even when she didn't fully understand me!

What a great teacher she was. She helped all of us in the family realize ourselves, supporting my father's quirky brand of Judaism, helping her children keep growing and changing and finding their identities. What love she had for me, and what respect she had for my faith, even though it differed from her own. What a beautiful kind of faith hers was, so graceful and open and giving.

CHAPTER TWO

PILGRIMS, TOURISTS, AND SEEKERS

Marrying Openness and Commitment

WE ALL FEEL AT ONE TIME OR ANOTHER THE DESIRE TO fall deeply into . . . what? Love? God? Faith? The Zone? We long to be certain of how to live, to know that we have found the right thing to which to commit ourselves. But all too often that commitment overwhelms us and blinds us and makes us forget that the thing to which we are deeply committed is not the only thing worthy of commitment. On the other hand, many of us can't seem to commit to anything at all. There seems to be too many choices, too many options, and by choosing one we will be denying ourselves all the others. Because we don't want to be narrow or dogmatic, we become disengaged. Because we want to stay open, we become disconnected and lonely.

I have come to think of the people in our society who are

unyieldingly committed as pilgrims, and of those who can't commit at all as tourists. Pilgrims know who they are and where they're going. Fundamentalists, many evangelicals, many orthodox Jews, jihadists, die-hard Democrats or Republicans, liberals and conservatives shouting back and forth at each other, ranting secularists, raving holy rollers—all are pilgrims. I know because I was one of them. I was walking in a direct line toward my sacred destination, and no one was going to get in my way.

During my senior year of high school in Chicago, I had decided that I wanted to go live in Israel and learn the Torah full-time. Although my parents were fiercely supportive of Israel, they would not have jumped for joy to learn that their seventeen-year-old son wanted to be a militant, ultrareligious Zionist warrior in the Holy Land rather than going to college. I imagined the conversations between my parents and their friends at Birchwood, our ritzy North Shore country club. Their friends would boast about their children, doing prelaw or premed at Ivy League schools. What would my parents say? Brad has just completed a new tractate of the Talmud and has a shiny new Kalashnikov that he is learning how to use and keeps loaded, under his bed.

So I contrived to be accepted at Yeshiva University, which had an affiliate in Jerusalem, Beit Midrash L'Torah, a modern orthodox institution with an overwhelmingly American student body and an overwhelmingly ultraorthodox Israeli faculty. My parents could say to their friends that their son was actually going to college, rather than naming what I was doing for what it was: returning to the Holy Land to live and reclaim—by any means necessary—the power and glory that had been Israel under kings David and Solomon.

We're not in Kansas anymore, Toto, I said to myself on the first morning after my arrival in Jerusalem, when I entered the yeshiva's dining room. About 250 boys with names like Shimi and Moish were sitting down to breakfast. Everyone knew everyone, except me. They had all attended a short list of New York City Jewish high schools. Even guys from Brooklyn knew the guys from Manhattan through athletic leagues and youth groups. They all knew what they were getting into. The yeshiva was not so different from their world in New York, and their older brothers and friends had gone through school here and reported back. I don't think that I have ever since felt such simultaneous excitement and uncertainty about a decision that I have reached.

We referred to our teachers during the day as the "morning rebbes," (a rebbe is a teacher or master, while *rabbi* denotes what has come to be a professional position). It was an affectionate name for the mostly middle-aged ultraorthodox men in big black hats and black suits with long beards who raised large families on small salaries for the privilege of immersing in the study and teaching of God's word. They were brilliant teachers, full of intellectual intensity. We focused on the Babylonian Talmud, a three-thousand-page collection of legal and biblical commentary organized around themes that ranged from prayer and property law to miracles and marriage. I don't know if it's practical to spend that much time figuring out what to do if your ox gores my ox—certainly neither I nor anyone there actually possessed an ox—but that was not the point. The Talmud is a two-thousand-year-old conversation in which we were being invited to participate. One of our teachers was fond of saying, "Remember, gentlemen, when you pray, God hears you; but when you learn, you can hear God!" And as a pilgrim, that was just what *I* wanted to hear.

The morning rebbes were, almost without exception, apolitical. They were devoted to books and learning, not borders or buildings. But at night the yeshiva was transformed. In came the militant Zionists with big knitted *kippot* and *payot,* long locks of hair at their temples, which they tucked behind their ears. They were even more intense than the morning rebbes. They taught the same thing as the morning rebbes, except with a different worldview. We not only studied the word of God with them, we participated in building the State of Israel. We fulfilled the biblical vision in which all Jews would one day return to their ancestral home, and they made us feel how privileged we were and what a responsibility we had to be living at that moment.

The morning rebbes taught us how to live according to the Torah; the night rebbes invited us to make the Torah come to life. The night rebbes were all connected to Rabbi Abraham Issac Kook's yeshiva, which was run by his son, Rabbi Tzvi Yehuda Kook. The elder Kook, who became the first chief Rabbi of Israel and who had died in 1935, was a mystic sage who wrote beautiful poetry and a Talmudic master who was known for the brilliant legal decisions he rendered. He had agreed, against the wishes of virtually every other Orthodox rabbi in the world, to work with the early Zionists, even though they were overwhelmingly secular, because he saw the sacred possibilities of building a Jewish state and the sacredness of the contribution of every Jew to making that happen, regardless of whether he or she was observant or nonobservant.

The night rebbes fervently believed that God wanted us to

expand Israel, to return not only to that territory, which had been offered by the United Nations in 1948, but to the territories promised by God to the ancient Israelites in the Bible—which include Gaza and the West Bank—that we had *recaptured* in the war of 1967.

That was what I'd come to Israel for: to participate in the holy task of reconstituting the Jewish state within its biblical borders. I was already a bit of a militant. At fourteen I had joined the Jewish Defense League in Chicago. Like most boys my age, I was looking for a cause, a team, and even a bit of a fight. The JDL was perfect for that. Although my parents hated its methods, they respected its desire to stand up for threatened Jews.

It wasn't such a big step for me from going with my parents, when the Bolshoi Ballet came to Chicago, to protest the Soviet Union's treatment of Jews, to trying to throw eggs at the dancers and smuggle smoke bombs into the performances with the JDL. I was arrested in a riot when the American Nazi Party held a rally in Skokie, Illinois, and I had a rib broken in a rumble at Northwestern University when we confronted a group of Palestinian students who were protesting Israeli prime minister Menachem Begin's visit to the campus.

The night rebbes quickly noticed my fiery political Judaism and gave me entrée into their world. I was flabbergasted, soon after my arrival at the yeshiva, when Kalman, an older student who was close to completing his rabbinic studies, asked if I would like to meet Rav Tzvi Yehuda. I couldn't believe my good fortune. It was like a seminarian being asked by a novice priest if he would like to meet the pope.

On a Saturday afternoon, Kalman brought me to Kook's

modest apartment. A young man with a crocheted *kippah* and a white shirt, buttoned at the collar, opened the door. He had blond hair, a blond beard, and blond *payot,* a postmodern Hasidic look that signified that he had embraced politics and power in a way that typical Hasidim never had while, at the same time, keeping the mystical connection that went back to Hasidism's founder, the Baal Shem Tov, a spiritual master from the eighteenth century who saw the wonder of God in everything.

The fact that Kook and son and their thousands of followers had embraced the holiness of every Jew (most of whom were overwhelmingly secular) who participated in the sacred work of building and maintaining Israel was one of the reasons that I had gravitated toward them. It didn't matter that my father had ordered up plates of ribs and shrimp at Ho Kow's, or that my mother had grown up with a Christmas tree in the house. Kook's way of thinking allowed me to be who I most wanted to be, while continuing to embrace my family, whom the morning rebbes would have condemned as having betrayed their identities, community, and destiny because they were not observant in the way we at the yeshiva were. By embracing Kook's ideology, I did not have to choose between being faithful to my tradition and being faithful to my family—which is too often the case when people embrace a new spiritual path.

Kook's apartment had two little rooms, a plain wooden table, and a narrow bed. He wore a long black coat and an enormous black velvet *kippah.* He had a flowing white beard and fierce eyes and was seated at the table, finishing the last Shabbat meal, half a roll. Even seated, I could see he was stooped. He reached up, and I grasped his hand. I spoke to him in the third person, which is the practice when addressing great teachers in the yeshiva world. "A good Shabbat to the honorable rabbi," I said. He gestured for me to sit down.

I was incredibly nervous. My mouth was dry and the words wouldn't come. I was afraid that I would offend him, embarrass myself, and make Kalman regret that he had brought me. I was sitting with the master of the movement to which I desperately wanted to belong. Needless to say, the meeting was far more significant to me than to him, and the conversation was brief.

"Where are you from?" Kook asked.

"Chicago, in America," I replied.

He looked at me. "But now you're home," he said. Those words bathed me in light and warmth and fanned the flames that were already burning inside me. To hear those words from his lips was a dream come true.

That was it. I rose to go.

"You'll come back later," Kook said to Kalman.

Kalman nodded.

"What did he mean?" I asked Kalman when we were out on the street.

"You'll see," Kalman replied.

We found a synagogue in the neighborhood to pray the evening service, then took a walk around the neighborhood. Kalman kept checking his watch. "Now it is time to go back," he finally said.

Kook's apartment was packed. Moshe Levinger, founder of the settlement community in Hebron, was there, along with Hanan Porat of Tehiya, a political party that was determined to settle every square inch of biblical Israel. I had heard Porat

speak in Chicago, and his presence further confirmed that this
was the place to be on this particular Saturday night. I had met
the pope; now I was pulling up a chair in the College of Cardinals.

My mouth was hanging open. "You don't say anything,"
Kalman said. "You just listen."

The energy in the room was unbelievable. All the things
that Jews had prayed for during all those years of exile were about
to happen. We were making them happen! Usually religion is
about making life conform to the page, but here the pages were
coming to life.

Kook was propped up in his bed, old and frail, talking to his
operatives, the heads of yeshivas and the leaders of the settlers'
political parties. He was giving them their marching orders.

I found myself standing before Yankele Levine, a rabbi
who had been ordained by Kook and worked for Ariel Sharon.

"Do you know Beit Hadassah?" Yankele asked me.

"Of course," I replied. "That's where Jewish people are re-
building Hebron."

Yankele seemed surprised that I knew what it was. "You
have to spend Shabbat there," he said. "I will set it up."

And that was how I took the next step in my pilgrimage. I
soon found myself on the way to Hebron—and once I was in
Hebron, I was hooked.

In those days you could hop on an Egged bus that traveled
between Jerusalem and Hebron. (Today the bus still runs, but
it's armored, the schedule is erratic, and it's a difficult trip because

of the increased hostility between Israel and the Palestinians.)
The bus drivers were often reluctant to take you all the way into
town. What Jew in his right mind would want to go to a place
where most everyone hated you and wished to do you harm?

"The army doesn't want me to go down into the city," the
driver would say as an excuse. But if you replied, "Okay, I'll
walk," the driver would respond, "No, no. That's okay. I'll take
you." Egged drivers, especially in those days, were usually
Sephardic men from places like Morocco and Tunisia with rough
exteriors and deeply protective impulses toward their passengers.

That first Shabbat in Hebron, we went to the cave of
Makhpelah to pray. It was a deeply moving experience for me,
and not because it was the first time I had been there. In 1973 I
had been to the Makhpelah with my family, and I went again in
1979 on a teen tour. But on both of these trips I was a tourist. I
was interested, I was titillated, I was even inspired. But then I left
Israel and went home and got on with my life. Not so that first
Shabbat. Even more than in the yeshiva in Jerusalem, even more
than in Kook's apartment, I was home. I was a pilgrim who had
finally reached his destination. I felt whole. Complete. This was
what God wanted. This was what God had commanded: Brad
Hirschfield, nice Jewish boy from the North Shore, standing at a
tomb in Hebron, surrounded by one hundred thousand Palestinians who hated my presence there, singing Hebrew prayers.

I know it may sound ridiculous now, but then I didn't question it for one moment. There was not an inkling of doubt.

I had come to Hebron in February of 1981 during a tense
time. In April 1980, Palestinians had attacked a group of Jewish

settlers who were returning to their homes from prayers on Friday night at the cave. Six young men were murdered by bullets and grenades; many more were injured. By the time I arrived in 1981, stabbings, stonings, and even shootings of settlers were an ongoing part of life.

That, of course, did not deter us. After prayers were over, we returned home not by the main street, the safest and most direct route, but by ecstatically dancing and singing our way through the kasbah, the market area of the city, a series of winding, narrow alleys. We wanted to proclaim our presence to the Arab population, to say that they were going to have to deal with us Jews.

Finally, when we had returned to Beit Hadassah, we danced for hours, singing one song over and over, *V'shavoo Banim L'gvoolam* ("Your Children Have Returned to Their Borders"), a line taken from the prophets.

We danced in the spot where recently the settlers had been murdered. We danced in very tight concentric circles, packed next to one another. I felt the centripetal force of the group; it was pushing me into its nucleus. But I didn't feel at all crowded. I felt liberated, safe, and warm—as if we were all one being. The movement and song were like a centrifuge, whirling and whirling, creating energy and power.

We danced on the stones where our blood had been spilled, proclaiming to the silent buildings around us and the city that hated us and the dark hills and the starlit sky—YOU CAN'T KILL US. WE WILL NEVER DIE.

I was ecstatic that night. I had never felt happier or more alive. Other than at my wedding, I have never danced like that.

Many of the roughly one hundred people who lived in Beit Hadassah came from comfortable homes, which they had given up to live eight in a room and subsist on tomatoes and pita. I came at a moment when many settlers had become increasingly frustrated with the army's inability to defend us, and were arguing for taking matters into their own hands. That was how the settlers' underground movement was born.

Despite being numerically small, the underground included a number of prominent rabbis and settler leaders. It began advocating for an increasingly harsh response against violence directed at Jews. It orchestrated the car bombings of West Bank mayors and plotted to blow up the Dome of the Rock in Jerusalem, a Muslim holy place and the site upon which the Jewish Temple had stood in ancient times.

Most of this made sense to me. Jews were being killed for settling in what had once been Jewish homes. This was our land, given to us by God.

For two years I gave myself over to Levinger and his group and the militant arm of the settlers' movement. When settlers Menachem Livni, Shauli Nir, and Uzi Sharabaf (whom I knew, although I was not in Hebron that day) fired into the Hebron Islamic College and killed two Palestinian children, I really felt sick. My reaction shocks me, in retrospect, given how easily I had dismissed the earlier attempts on the lives of various Palestinian mayors. The deaths of those children crossed some internal line in me. Such lines for all of us are unknown and unknowable until we reach them, but once they're crossed, our whole world begins to look different.

. No one felt good about what had happened. Most of my group felt it was a tragic mistake, but they also thought it a natural result of continuous violence against us and a lack of a forceful response by the army. *No one* questioned the wisdom of building the Hebron community in light of what had happened.

I found myself outside the fold. I stopped going to Hebron. I had no idea how to discuss how I felt with anyone within the settlers' movement. And I had no desire to talk to anyone outside about it, either. I simply wanted to put it away and forget it. I was no longer a pilgrim. I didn't quite know what I was.

In all the years between the shooting of those Palestinian schoolgirls and that sunny morning when I watched the planes slam into the Twin Towers, I had avoided talking about my Hebron experience. Israel had caught and jailed the men who shot the Palestinian girls, and I had gone on to college and graduate school and been ordained as a rabbi after being pressed and inspired by my students.

I became an intern at a place called CLAL, the National Jewish Center for Learning and Leadership, which had been founded in 1973 by Rabbi Irving Yitz Greenberg—a towering intellect, prolific author, and enormously influential figure in the Jewish world—to nurture the spiritual dignity of all kinds of Judaism. Yitz's basic thinking was that after the Holocaust, in which Jews had all died together, regardless of what kind of Jews they were, we needed to learn to live together, in spite of our differing ideologies and responses to our heritage. I found that idea both moving and exciting. I saw in Yitz's teachings the beginnings of an approach that recalibrated the way we thought about right and wrong and truth and falsehood. I felt the kind of deep commitment to truth and leading a spiritual life that I had felt in Hebron, with a new openness and sense of inclusion.

I stayed on at CLAL and eventually became its president, along with my dear friend and intellectual soul mate, Rabbi Irwin Kula. As I developed my own thinking, I became committed to using Jewish thought to address universal or human questions. I think Judaism's ancient tradition can help *all* people find deeper meaning and greater joy in their lives, whether or not they are Jewish. I have come to believe that religious traditions exist not to serve the faithful, but to help the faithful serve the world. The traditions are there for anyone to use to craft his or her life.

The events of 9/11 made me realize that I needed to confront my own past, because through all the years I had been back in the United States, I had never discussed what happened to me in Hebron with anyone. I knew it was time to exhume the experience and examine it publicly. Religion had flown those planes into the Twin Towers, and I had practiced a form of that religion. It is the religion of pilgrims, of people who see no way but their own way, and treat people who do not support them as mistakes that need to be erased.

I am not drawing a moral equivalence between the average Jewish resident of Hebron and the murderers of 9/11. Still, the painful reality is that we shared an absolute sense of our own way of being right that made everyone else wrong. That situation is not limited to such extreme situations. It's endemic in our society, which has become increasingly polarized between what I have come to think of as pilgrims and tourists, and I believe there must be another way to live, a way that marries openness and commitment, that says you don't have to be wrong for me to be right, that can find and practice a faith that does not slip into fanaticism, even if that fanaticism is subtle and covert. I have come to think of that approach to life as *seeking*.

When I was a pilgrim in Hebron, I had little use for tourists, beyond getting them to become pilgrims, or at least to support our pilgrimage, although after I departed from the pilgrim's path I was able to admit to myself that being a tourist can be a whole lot of fun. Nevertheless, I still knew that as tourists we aren't truly invested in our journeys. They are hiatuses, breaks from real life and its commitments, struggles, and difficulties.

The symbol of the tourist is the camera. We take cameras on trips to record experiences that are out of the ordinary, which is great. But when we start feeling at home in a place, we no longer feel the need to capture the experience in the same way. When we travel we find ourselves capturing images of our fellow travelers, more than the things that we are seeing on the trip. It becomes part of our everyday life, part of who we are. That's when tourism begins to shift into something else. We are no longer superficial transients. We start imagining that the journey on which we find ourselves at that particular moment will affect us far into the future, that the experiences will shape our thoughts and actions long after we have left this place or that place behind. Seeking is about realizing that the journey has not ended, but that each place in which you find yourself demands attention and commitment.

The biblical journey of Abraham provides an ancient model for the principals of seeking. There are three key moments in Abraham's journey.

Abraham sets out from his home, from everything he knows, when God calls to him and says, "Go to the land that I will show you." Abraham does not know exactly where he is going. That is the first principal of seeking—to get moving, even if you only have a direction, not a destination.

We must never worry that we are not up to the task, although most of us always will. After all, who was Abraham? What was special about him? Nothing! Abraham and Sarah were you and me. Rabbinic commentaries pad the biblical account with legends of Abraham's wisdom, bravery, and strength in order to justify his election by God. But I think the whole point of the story, which has none of those details, is to help each of us realize that we can be them.

Abraham doesn't know where he's going. In Hebron, I knew exactly where I was going. My journey was entirely comfortable for me. Unlike Abraham and Sarah, I wanted to be comfortable, while they were content to be safe. That might be a good way to sum up the entire challenge before us right now. People long to be comfortable because they feel unsafe, but if we could help people to feel safe, then they could risk being uncomfortable. It is a paradox that the pursuit of comfort, of certainty, makes us unsafe, both to others and to ourselves. The real issue is how to help people feel safe enough to risk being uncomfortable and uncertain. God did that for Abraham and Sarah, and it is to that kind of safety that our journeys must lead. The first principle of any spiritual tradition or any great relationship is to make us feel so loved and safe that we are willing to risk a little uncertainty and discomfort, because whatever happens, we know that the tradition or the other person will really be there for us.

Abraham wandered circuitously. But all the places he stopped on his journey, all the fits and starts, the misadventures and misdirection, were sacred. They were all part of the process. There is no straight line in spiritual growth, in genuine seeking, in the journey. We don't have to be angry with people who are still in places that we have stopped along the way, but from which we have since moved on. There is also no reason to feel ashamed of the places from which we come. If we had not made those stops along the way, we would not be where or who we are now.

Movement is the first sacred principal. Whenever you think you've reached the end, there's always more up ahead. There's always more meaning and purpose than we can possibly imagine. The Hebrew word for heaven, *olam habah,* is usually translated as "the world to come," as if heaven is fixed. But it also translates as "the world that is coming"—a moving, dynamic place where we will face a new set of challenges and opportunities.

Mutuality is the second sacred principal of the seeker. In Abraham's journey, when God says he plans to destroy Sodom, Abraham asks, "Will you sweep away innocent along with guilty?" In essence, Abraham is telling God that if God surrenders a sense of justice and goodness, then God isn't God.

What a teaching this is! The Bible is telling us that sometimes the height of impiety is a moment of profound religious insight. Arguing with God—*rejecting* God—can be as sacred as accepting God. There are times when not believing in God is as holy as believing in God with all your heart and soul. One of the lessons of the Sodom story is that Abraham, the Bible's first monotheist, is also the Bible's first atheist.

There are many days when I'm praying in my tallis, a long woolen prayer shawl, and *tefillin,* small hard leather boxes that I wear on my head and my left arm (uniting my head and heart in prayer), that I, like Abraham, cry out to God at the injustice and violence in the world. I am profoundly angry at God, and I believe with all my heart that sometimes shouting at God is as important as accepting God.

The tallis and *tefillin* are tokens of the relationship between us. I know they don't mean anything in and of themselves, but they are symbols, like my wedding ring (and I know if I lost my wedding ring where I'd be sleeping tonight). These tokens count, in part, because they are reminders that you are so connected you can say anything to each other. Abraham can say to God (and we can say to the people we love): you're done being you if you insist on doing what you're doing, and I love you too much to let you do that.

Atheists can be more religious than I am. For Abraham to be ready to walk away from a God that *pretends* to be just and decent is a profoundly spiritual act. But we also have to realize as seekers that in rejecting God, in rejecting belief, we can be just as static, dogmatic, and self-affirming as pilgrims.

After Abraham tells God that He's a malevolent SOB if He wipes out the city, God says okay, if I can find fifty righteous people I'll spare Sodom. Abraham negotiates with God, bringing the number down from fifty to forty-five, to forty, to thirty, to twenty, and finally to ten. As he begins this process of negotiation, Abraham says to God, "How can I speak, I am nothing but dust and ashes." The Bible shows us that the act of maximum audacity in negotiating with God also demands maximum humility.

I try to keep that lesson close to me. When Becky and I fight, I always try to accept, deep inside myself, that no matter how passionately I feel about the position I'm taking, I may be completely wrong. I work hard to recognize that no matter how puffed up and self-righteous I may feel, I am nothing compared to a woman who has given birth to my children and loved me so steadfastly with such an open heart all these years.

Why does Abraham stop bargaining with God at ten good people? What if there were only nine people who passed muster and you were one of those nine?

I think one of the things the Bible may be teaching us is that there are always limits to how far you can push the people you love, that there needs to be a balance between being able to say anything and to know when to stop pushing. This point is amplified in the story's ending. The Bible says that when the Lord had finished talking to Abraham, God departed. Abraham has done most of the talking in this conversation, and he has clearly come out on top. It would be more apt for the story to say that God departed when Abraham had finished talking to Him.

There is wisdom in this reversal. Perhaps the Bible is telling us that it's important not to gloat, which is our tendency when we win an argument. We feel smug and self-satisfied. In our relationships and politics and religion, when we have made our point and come out on top, it's vitally important to protect the dignity of the person or position we have bested.

True seeking encourages arguing and fighting; it embraces testing and dispute, but only on the condition that the dignity of both sides is retained. That is mutuality: whoever appears to be less powerful should be encouraged to exert power and should be protected.

I try to drive this lesson home with my children. Avi and Dassi, my two older daughters, can never agree on where to go for pizza. I make sure that whoever wins the inevitable argument that ensues whenever we want pizza makes sure that her sister is served first and gets something that she likes. In the case of Avi, that's a cheese calzone, which Judean Hills, the pizza shop that makes the pizza she doesn't like, only makes on certain days. Dassi has to call Judean Hills to find out if they have calzones before we go there, otherwise we go to Main Event, the other pizza place. It's vitally important to me that my daughters learn that when they win an argument, the loser gets something that may not be ideal, but is at least acceptable. Moreover, the winner must be careful to provide it, or she doesn't deserve to win.

This principal is not just about pizza. The stronger Israel is, the more committed I am to creating Palestine. This is not for the Palestinians—it's for me! We have to be very clear about what our obligations are when we get what we want. That's what it means to be an ethical, powerful person.

The last step in God's relationship with Abraham that points us on the path of seeking is mitzvah, which is usually

defined as a good deed or religious act. That is the surface meaning of individual mitzvoth: specific, single acts of goodness or
observance. Mitzvah, however, is much more than that. It's a
human capacity.

When God calls out to Abraham, Abraham responds with
the Hebrew word *hineini*—"Here I am." This is mitzvah. It's how
you feel when your sick kid wakes up in the middle of the night
and you have to get up the next morning to go to work. "Here I
am," you say to your child, no matter how tired you are. We all
need mitzvah in our lives, or life becomes shallow, disconnected,
without meaning. We need to feel able to be there for the people
we love and the things in which we deeply believe, which we hold
sacred.

Our capacity to say "Here I am" is tied to the feeling that
other people will say it to us. I know that in the middle of the
night when one of our daughters wakes up sick, Becky will say
hineini for me. For us to be truly strong, we need someone who
is giving us strength. When my father had a stroke and I flew
out to California to be there for my mother, I was able to do that
because a friend drove two hours to be there for me.

We always need to be in both positions, demanding the
hineini response from ourselves and demanding for ourselves that
others say it to us. When it's either one or the other, we get into
ruts. If you're always giving it, you get burned out and resentful.
When you're always demanding it without giving it, you're selfish and immature.

Mitzvah is a crucial principal in the journey of the seeker.
When Abraham says "Here I am," he is saying, "I am present, I
am fully here, how can I help?" It doesn't matter where we apply

that in our lives, to our children or to God, as long as we live that way and have that response to the sacred parts of our lives.

Abraham says *hineini* without knowing exactly where he is going or what will be asked from him. He is a seeker on a journey. He is not a tourist, always on the outside looking in, at a remove from life. He isn't a pilgrim, a fanatic trudging along with his eyes fixed on some distant point. He embodies the marriage of openness and commitment.

When we're really open—*that* is when we're ready to feel more and to be more. We will be able to get moving and wander without being sure where we will end up or what will be asked of us. We will feel safe, but we won't necessarily always feel comfortable. We will be able to protect the dignity of those who are weaker than we are. We will be able to see that doubt can be as sacred as belief. We will be able to say "Here I am" when we wake each morning to continue on the journeys that are our lives. We will be able to marry commitment and openness and begin each day seeking afresh.

CHAPTER THREE

THE SHADOW SIDE
OF FAITH

Learning That We Can Be Both

Victims and Victimizers

MY MOTHER'S FAITH WAS EXTRAORDINARY, AS WAS MY GREAT-grandmother's. Each of them understood in her own way that faith should always empower and be an inspiration. But we all know that faith isn't always like that. Too often, faith becomes the ground from which we lash out, from which we justify that which we already believe, rather than the place inside ourselves from which we find the strength to become seekers and open ourselves to new people and new ideas. There is a shadow side to deep faith, a terrifying face of faith that almost demands that we walk away from faith altogether and completely renounce it.

That is precisely what Sam Harris, in his book *The End of Faith,* would have us do. "We must find a way to a time when faith," writes Harris, "without evidence, disgraces anyone who would claim it. Given the present state of the world, there appears to be no other future worth wanting. It is imperative that we begin speaking plainly about the absurdity of most of our religious beliefs."

We can walk away from faith because it is absurd (ridiculous at best, dangerous at worst) and leads people to fly planes into buildings and blow themselves up in the name of God. Or we can grapple with the reality of what it means to be human. Faith is wrapped into our history, values, aspirations, and dreams. Because faith can be irrational and extreme is no reason to think we should evolve beyond it, any more than we might think that we should—or could—evolve beyond our capacity for love. Love can also be terrible or wonderful, creative and life-affirming or soul-shattering and suicidal. We don't walk away from love because it defies reason. And we shouldn't walk away from faith, either.

All the arguments about losing faith after one sees faith's terrible face seem to me like deciding to eat only raw food after you turn on a burner and accidentally burn down the house. Faith is a fire that burns inside us: it can be used for both good and ill. What we need to do, especially today, is to wrestle with the meaning of the terrible face of faith and learn from it.

One of the most pernicious reflexes of the shadow side of faith is to turn victims into victimizers. You don't have to be a holy roller or a Hasidic Jew to do this—it's a common human tendency and it's not limited to religion. That's how children who are abused become abusive parents. What effort it takes to break that cycle!

It seems to be my fate to bump against this particular expression of the shadow side of faith. I can't seem to escape it, and so I was only faintly surprised when I was asked to comment on the case of Karin Robidoux for Court TV, the cable television channel.

Karin was a member of The Body, a small but fanatical cult in Bedford, Massachusetts. Her sister-in-law, Michelle Mingo, received a prophecy—what the group called a "leading"—from God, which was verified by Body founder, Roland Robidoux, Karin's father-in-law. The "leading" instructed Karin to subsist on small amounts of almond milk, and briefly nurse her ten-month-old baby, Samuel, twice a day. Karin quickly became malnourished and Samuel, who was already eating solid food, died of starvation nine days before his first birthday.

I watched the taped proceedings of Karin's trial, which took place in Bedford in 2004, in one of Court TV's midtown Manhattan studios. Karin was a dejected woman in her twenties who had grown up in a Catholic working-class family in Bedford. Broken and forlorn, she projected none of the self-righteousness of someone who believes that she has done God's will.

Our world is made up of perpetrators and victims, argued the prosecuting attorney, and Karin had perpetrated the terrible crime of starving Samuel. The world *is* divided between perpetrators and victims, said the defense attorney. But Karin was innocent, the hapless victim of a manipulative husband and an extremist cult.

The host asked for my thoughts, and I tried to introduce a

third perspective: a person can be both a perpetrator and a victim. I said that if Karin was found guilty, then the prosecutor should get up and say yes, she has been victimized, and you should cry for her but still find her accountable for killing her child. Compassion and understanding don't rule out justice. If we can't hold that possibility in our minds, then we are doomed to an endless cycle of people claiming they are victims in order to justify victimizing others.

The Bible is filled with stories of characters who are both victims and victimizers. In the Book of Genesis, Joseph is sold into slavery in Egypt, but then becomes an enslaver as Pharaoh's Head of the Court. In the next generation, the Israelites become slaves to a new Pharaoh: the cycle of enslavement continues. Freed by Moses hundreds of years later, the newly liberated Israelites embed enslavement in their experience of freedom.

The memory of past oppression can break two ways in our lives. It can make us resentful and full of reasons why now it's someone else's turn to suffer as we have; and it can soften our hearts and open our eyes to suffering. It can deepen our commitment to help others as we wish others had helped us. Turning personal or national suffering into a source for healing is never easy, but unless that remains our top priority, we'll be left with a world in which everybody has a finely honed sense of how his particular past entitles him to undermine someone else's future.

In the Book of Esther, the king's chief minister, Haman, plots to destroy all the Jews (men, women, and children) living in the Persian Empire in the third century B.C.E. But when Queen Esther, who is Jewish, persuades King Ahasuerus to reconsider, the king hangs Haman, and gives Esther and her fellow Jews permission to kill their enemies—75,000 people. The victims of a genocidal conspiracy become the perpetrators of their own brand of violent cleansing. The victims become the victimizers. I mean, let's face it: no Jews had been killed yet. Of what were those 75,000 Persians guilty? Being prepared to kill Jews? Apparently the impulse that turns victims into victimizers is so powerful that the author of the story could not imagine an ending to this tale without the reader being reassured that the hatred the Jews suffered would be returned in kind.

But even here the Bible has planted a seed that might grow into a solution and break the vicious cycle of hatred and retribution. Haman, we learn in the first chapters of the story, is a descendant of Esau, Jacob's twin brother and the progenitor of the Amalekites, just as Jacob is the progenitor of the Israelites. The paradigmatic "evildoer" (whose name is drowned out with noisemakers when the Book of Esther is read in synagogue on Purim) is actually a cousin of those whom he wished to destroy and who ultimately destroyed him! Victim and victimizer are related. Haman was trying to destroy his own family; he just couldn't see it. When Jews cheer Haman's death, we are cheering for the death of one of our own.

In a more just and forgiving world we would realize that the people who hurt us have often been hurt themselves. We would remember that those against whom we struggle are actually "us," not some wholly other "them." It's not that we would never have to fight against certain people and specific things. We would. But how would those fights be different, how much more slowly would they be entered into and how much more quickly resolved if all those involved acknowledged that their intended victims were their own relatives, and they were actually fighting against themselves? What would war look like if we felt obliged to remember the names of the "enemy" dead alongside our own, not because we believed that they were fighting for the right side, but because however wrong they were, they were part of our family?

The jury acquitted Karin Robidoux of murder, finding her guilty on a single count of battery. She was sentenced to prison for two years, the maximum sentence for that crime, but was immediately released because she hadn't been able to make bail upon arrest and had already spent two years behind bars, awaiting trail.

In a prior trial in 2002, Karin's husband, Jacques, had been found guilty of first-degree murder and sentenced to life in prison without parole because the jury felt he had manipulated Karin into complying with her sister-in-law's "leading" to starve Samuel.

The jury in Karin's case, I think, felt that they had already found their perpetrator in Jacques, and it was far easier for them to exonerate Karin than to convict her. Karin, like all of us, had someone else at whom she could point her finger and say, "It's not my fault—he made me do it." Once we point that finger, we assume we're no longer responsible. In showing how someone else is the victimizer, we establish for ourselves the safety of the status of victim—the perfect dodge.

It's not that all of us are equally guilty—we're not. Not all our mistakes or bad acts are equally serious. When I have had a bad day and can't find the time, energy, or patience to relate to my kids in the way that I know I should, or talk to my wife with the warmth and focus that I want her to have when she talks to me, that's not abuse, but it's not okay, either. Is it understandable? Of course (at least I hope so)! A reasonable explanation, such as tension at work, should not become an excuse for failing to improve my behavior, but it is something that Becky and the girls should take into account to soften their response to my failings.

You can say to those you love, "You've hurt me, and I understand why." You can make the space inside yourself to realize that reality is big enough to contain simultaneously both the love you feel for them and an honest accounting of the hurt they've done you. Love is *not* about never having to say you're sorry. The opposite is true: genuine love makes it possible to say I'm sorry and to know that together you'll move on from that place.

When I am victimizing Becky, she can still empathize, understanding that I have been victimized. When I recognize that I am victimizing, I need to realize that I should be a little more careful. When she recognizes that I have been victimized, she needs to be a little gentler. Instead, we usually run for cover with a good excuse. We assume that because our behavior can be explained, it is acceptable. Meanwhile the person on the receiving end of our impatience, insensitivity, or downright cruelty focuses only on his or her own hurt, afraid that understanding will facilitate repetition.

Abnegating guilt and reneging on personal responsibility is *always* dangerous. So, too, is the fear that forgiveness will lead to forgetfulness or moral insensitivity. But that is what we do when we divide the world into victims and victimizers. We move quickly to identify the bad guys and the good guys, laying all blame at the feet of the first and assuming perfect innocence for the second. It's hard to imagine we can be both, but in almost every circumstance we are. Joseph and Esther are heroic figures, but the Bible doesn't whitewash their story. They are both victims and victimizers, and it's up to us to evaluate whether their balancing act is successful. That complexity is the stuff of real spiritual growth, of religious wisdom that endures and is worth preserving and learning from.

M y thinking about victims and victimizers began one beautiful spring day soon after I started going to Hebron. I was with the son-in-law of Rabbi Moshe Levinger, the leader of the community, at the Makhpelah. Levinger and his core group of followers were heroes to me, and I aspired to be just like them.

We had just finished praying the afternoon service with a group of visiting American students and had stayed on to study in one of the small rooms above the tomb that functioned as a synagogue in the midst of what had come to be a mosque. The only reason we were allowed to have a synagogue inside the mosque was the Israeli army's presence in Hebron.

Our presence *inside* the mosque, over the cave and its tombs, was especially powerful for us. When Hebron had been under control of the Ottoman Empire and then the British, there had been the Rule of the Seventh Step: Jews were allowed to walk only to the seventh of the steps that led into the mosque, but no farther. They were allowed to peer down the hall of the mosque to the tomb, but not go in.

Being in the Makhpelah was always a powerful experience

for me, not only because of its holiness as the burial ground of Abraham, Sarah, Isaac, Rebecca, Jacob, and Leah. It was at the center of the place from which we made the claim that God's word was alive, the promise that Jews would take possession of the entire land of Israel, something that we were making happen by our presence there. I was seventeen years old, and I was proving a point, and it felt great!

This is exactly the kind of faith that Harris would call with some justification destructive and deluded. But it also encompassed a deep feeling of connection, purpose, history, and meaning. It was a beautiful and powerful way to live. And I still feel that today, even after all that has happened.

In front of the tomb was a large plaza that was a popular gathering place, busy with people shopping at peddlers' pushcarts. It served as an entrance to the kasbah.

A commotion ensued as Levinger's son-in-law and I left the tomb on our way back into the city. The Palestinian crowd in the plaza thought a Jewish settler had overturned a vendor's pushcart. In 1981 in Hebron, it was entirely possible that a settler had, indeed, spitefully done just that, or that the cart had been overturned by a Palestinian who then started screaming, "The Jews did it!" Jewish-Palestinian relations were that toxic.

The crowd coalesced, its anger mounting. I was both apprehensive—there were many more of them than of us—and furious. Settlers were murdered for simply walking the streets of "our" city, and Palestinians frothed at the mouth over a fruit cart! It was outrageous. Offensive.

Israeli soldiers nearby soon made their presence felt, deploying through the plaza in riot gear. With the implicit threat of tear gas and rubber-coated bullets, the crowd cooled. I was immensely relieved. A near riot had been defused, and I thought this was a happy ending to what could have easily become a bloody mess.

In 1981 in Hebron, Jewish civilians, myself included, never went out without a weapon. The three most popular were 9-mm pistols, Uzis, and Kalashnikov assault rifles. Training to use them was a fairly straightforward process: we spent a day at a range, firing them under military supervision.

I noticed, as the crowd dispersed and everything returned to its normal state of wary equilibrium, that my companion was incensed.

"What's wrong?" I asked.

"It jammed," he spat. "These Uzis never jam."

And it was true, they didn't. If anything they had a tendency to fire when you didn't want them to.

With a sickening rush I realized that my companion had been trying to cock his gun to use on the crowd. It dawned on me that we Jews, who I considered to be the ultimate victims, were in danger of becoming victimizers.

To be sure, it may seem that this realization was a little late in coming, even for someone so young. But try to understand my frame of mind. I felt every Jew had a right to live anywhere in the biblical land of Israel, under Jewish sovereignty. The exile of the Jews from their biblical birthright for the last two thousand years, all the persecution that the Jewish people had endured, culminating in the Holocaust, had given us, as victims, the absolute right to come home to Tel Aviv, Jerusalem, and Hebron.

Nevertheless, I glimpsed the cost of that way of thinking,

and from that moment forward I made a decision not to carry my weapon unless I was on guard duty or leading an American tour group in Hebron. Someone whom I held in great esteem had mourned the lost opportunity to do serious violence. I, too, had felt the seductive draw of wanting to lash out, to become the victimizer. You don't think of yourself as victimizing anyone. You think you're defending yourself, recovering lost power and redressing past wrongs. It *feels* right!

Of course, we couldn't have known then that thirteen years later (on Purim!) Dr. Baruch Goldstein would burst into a Hebron mosque and kill twenty-nine people and injure 150 others. Perhaps we should have known that it was just a matter of time until that or something like that happened, and that the only real question was whether we were okay with it or not.

There was no one I could talk with about the incident in the plaza. At best, the people inside the settler community would have said it was God's will that the Uzi had jammed. No one would have empathized with my queasiness. Still, the overwhelming feeling that I shared with the other settlers in Hebron was joy. We were often in an ecstatic state, possessed by the fathomless beauty of our cause, a rhapsodic mood that came from walking where Abraham had walked. In my heart I knew that something was off, but I was possessed.

A year later I was protesting the Israeli disengagement from Sinai, the last phase of the Sadat-Begin peace plan. I had stationed myself in Yamit, a small but very beautiful city on the Mediterranean coast just south of Gaza.

Yamit was the only place where Jews were still living in Sinai, and the place where we hoped to make a last stand. I was up to my old tricks, wrapped in a tallit, fasting and praying and ardently believing that if enough Jews did likewise, God would reverse the democratically elected government of Israel's decision to give up territory that God had promised to the Jewish people.

It made perfect sense—to us. We were plugged into the underlying logic of the unfolding plan that God had for mankind and God's chosen people. We felt the same way that the Robidouxs felt when they heard God telling them to starve little Samuel. We were above the rules that "mere people" created: God made our rules.

We plotted what we would do when the Israeli army arrived to evict us forcibly from Yamit. We thought of ourselves as victims, suffering over the loss of our sacred land.

Even in an asylum there is someone all the other inmates thinks is *really* crazy. In Yamit, that honor belonged to a group of Rabbi Meir Kahane's followers who occupied a bomb shelter and rigged its door with explosives. Israeli soldiers were the only people who would try to open that door.

The strategy of Kahane's group followed victim logic: once you do such-and-such to us, we're entitled to do *anything* to you.

I am ashamed to admit that it was the potential of this Jew-against-Jew violence—rather than the Jew against Muslim violence outside the tomb—that turned my queasiness into outright nausea. In Jewish tradition, all human life is equal. I should have known that the settler community of which I was a part was coming off its wheels the moment it started acting as if one human life was more valuable than another.

The shooting in Hebron of those Palestinian schoolgirls soon after Yamit completely undid me. "You are right, the shooting was problematic," said one rabbi to me. "But not fundamentally so." I couldn't believe what I was hearing.

My parents had nurtured my own journey despite serious misgivings about parts of it. But the spiritual guides with whom I was coming into contact saw no good in questions that challenged their own practices and perceptions. For them (and for me, too, until that moment), Jews had suffered for thousands of years. That others would endure some suffering on our way to fulfilling God's plan was of little consequence. Our status as the world's ultimate victims—Hitler's primary targets, the people who had wandered the world for two thousand years without a home—had hardened our hearts to the real cost of realizing our dreams.

M y Hebron experience helped me see the mistake we make when we use our feeling of having been the victim to wash off our role as victimizer, and it was from this very personal perspective that I made my comments on Karin's role in Samuel's death to the moderator on Court TV.

Then the moderator introduced another topic with which I have struggled since my *bubbe* tore my *kippah* off my head. "This isn't a real religion," the moderator said, referring to The Body. "Isn't it a cult?" He was drawing a distinction between "real religions," which are acceptable, and "cults," which are wicked.

I wish it were that simple.

I have had some of my most powerful spiritual experiences

as part of a community that many people would consider a cult, while some of my most spiritually deadening experiences have occurred in more "normal" Jewish religious settings. I knew that I needed to choose my words carefully or I would do something that I desperately did not want to do: deny the beauty of parts of so-called cult communities or minimize the potential ugliness of mainstream religion.

The distinction between cults and religions is far less clear-cut than most people think. The way we define a cult can't be based on its age. All religions have a starting point; each tradition was once an innovation. When early Jews proclaimed there was one God, and early Christians said Jesus was His only begotten son, their contemporaries thought they were lunatic cultists.

Cults do exist, and they have certain characteristics. They treat questions about the beliefs of the group as a challenge to their authority and authenticity. Doubt among their members is viewed as a sign of weakening faith and a lack of commitment to the cause. Cults typically cut off or strictly structure interactions outside their group. They teach that people who do not share their beliefs are living in darkness and are dangerous or corrosive. Cults set up a painful dichotomy between maintaining relationships with those inside the group, and losing them because one no longer shares the group's beliefs and practices.

Mainstream religions can behave in exactly the same way. I have friends who were raised in the Hasidic communities of New York and Jerusalem, and who are not allowed to see their childhood friends or even their own children because they have left the Hasidic way of life. I have a Catholic colleague who is not invited to his family's Christmas and Easter gatherings because

he is gay. How many people have ended their religious education when a minister, priest, or rabbi has told them that they
were asking "the wrong questions" instead of learning "the right
answers." How many of us have sat through a sermon in a
church, synagogue, or mosque in which we have heard that the
practice of some other faith is dangerous or deluded?

Should we brand all religious cults and simply walk away?
I have an older brother, an accomplished physician and scientist,
who thinks so, and perhaps he is right. But I am not ready to
give up just yet. Religious communities help you go beyond yourself to care for other people. They help sustain relationships
through terrible disappointments. As much as religion inspires
acts of terror and viciousness, it still inspires you to go beyond
yourself because you believe that there's something beyond you.
What causes such ugly behavior, whether in the name of religion
or of cults, is fear. Fear is always what's behind trying to preserve
what one perceives as the truth in a coercive, threatening way.

Groups with at least some of the characteristics of cults
often do the best job of caring for people. That was certainly the
case for Karin Robidoux, who had been thrown out of her home
by her parents. A secular social worker or liberal democrat didn't
take her in. Jacques Robidoux and The Body made room for a
young woman with no means of support.

The Body is not an anomaly. The Catholic Church has
grown to over 1.4 billion members using the same methods.
Hezbollah and Hamas are committed to materially helping their
many poor members. So is Shas, the Sephardic ultraorthodox
party in Israel. These groups are not morally equivalent, but they
have all done a much better job of caring for the most vulnerable

people in their midst than have many of their more broad-minded counterparts. Is building constituencies their only motive? Could it be that we need to accept that the same fanatical systems that produce some of the world's greatest pain also wisely produce the remedies to some of the world's most persistent problems?

When we consider what drives people to fanaticism, it's too easy to say that they glom on to God or become part of an insular group to validate or justify their miserable existence. Richard Dawkins, the scientist and author of *The God Delusion,* says faith is evidence of an underdeveloped mind. I would ask Dawkins: Do we have friends or lovers because we're insufficient, because of an absence of education, or because we're economically disadvantaged? Dawkins's argument is materialistic, akin to Marx's statement that religion is the opiate of the masses. All the explaining away along those lines doesn't account for the power of maintaining an intimate relationship with the source of all wisdom and life, whether that is called God, Allah, Adonai, spirit, or source.

Spiritual intimacy is a real experience, and I am moved that we live in a world where people have that kind of access. It's beautiful. But too often it is only the fanatical fringe that is committed to the notion that *all* of us are capable of and entitled to that kind of intimacy—direct communication and communion with the ultimate. It's sad that little cults are often more spiritually democratic than supposedly safe and well-established religions! But there's nothing new about that.

The Book of Numbers tells us of Eldad and Meidad, whose names in Hebrew mean "to the breast" and "from the breast." They ran through the Jewish camp in Sinai, prophesying in the name of God. Joshua, Moses' protégé, angrily reported this "obvious challenge" to his master's religious authority. "I wish that all the people of the Lord would be prophets and the Lord would put spirit upon them," Moses replied.

Instead of feeling threatened, Moses is excited by the possibility of free-flowing spiritual intuition, whatever its impact on his position. That does not mean we should go back to the era of prophets. But imagine if today's religious leaders could lead in their spirit. Moses knew that those young men were literally drinking in the milk of God. They were living examples that before God there are no spiritual runts who should be pushed off the breast.

I don't want to return to Hebron, and I have no interest in hanging out with Jacques Robidoux, or returning to the times of Joseph and Esther. But I don't want to leave them behind, either. There is beauty in all of them, and my ability to hold on to that is what keeps my life in balance, what keeps me from swinging from one extreme to the other, intoxicated by each without ever integrating the best that each has to offer. False dichotomies between victim and victimizer or cult and religion divide our loyalties between the people and ideas with which we are comfortable and those from which we can grow. When that happens, we all suffer. When it doesn't, we blossom.

CHAPTER FOUR

VENGEANCE, FORGIVENESS, JUSTICE, AND MERCY

Recognizing the Sacredness of

All Our Feelings

IN JUNE 2006, ABOUT A YEAR AFTER MY COURT TV APPEARANCE, I was invited to the Fes Festival of World Sacred Music in Morocco. During that year, Karin's case had resonated inside me as I watched events unfold around the world. America's war continued in Iraq; Israel disengaged from Gaza. In both cases, the sides for and against military action were passionate and divisive, claiming that they were victims and inevitably ending up as victimizers. Each side insisted that it was right and that the other side was wrong. What happened to The Body in Bedford, Massachusetts, was a microcosm of the larger world of politics and military force.

I learned that Faouzi Skali, a successful young Moroccan businessman raised in an upper-class Muslim home, had founded the festival. Skali had become a Sufi, a member of the mystical branch of Islam. He had wondered what to do with what he had been given, both in response to his privileged background and the Sufi tradition that he followed. *Wahdat,* or unity, is central to Sufi wisdom, and following the Sufi path is ultimately about allowing love to overcome all dualities.

Of course, that belief is itself a bit dualistic, dividing the world between the true and unified and the falsely dualistic. Personally, I believe that a serious commitment to unity would leave room for duality. Whether I am right or wrong about that, I am certain that a world in which more of us walked Faouzi's path, whatever we called it, would be a better place.

Skali founded the festival on the premise that music could take us to sacred places that ideas couldn't reach. I can relate. My heart opens when I hear certain songs, "Friend of the Devil" by the Grateful Dead, for example, which reconnects me to the years I spent at Camp Northstar in Hayward, Wisconsin, and the friends I made there. When I hear that song, I am able to work out of that consciousness. The lullaby written to accompany bedtime prayers written by Rabbi Shlomo Carlebach for his daughters, which I sang to mine when they were younger, I sing again softly to myself when I am trying to be a better father. That's how music works and why Skali created the festival.

When I first received the invitation, I wondered why in the world I had been invited. I'm not a musician or composer. Although I enjoy singing, I have short, stumpy fingers and, to my enormous frustration and regret, I have never been able to play piano or guitar.

Skali wanted to merge the "heart world" of music with

the "head world" of frank conversation about how to bridge the gaps between the world's religious traditions. I had been invited to speak at the Colloquium, which was meant to facilitate the kinds of conversations on how to unify people around the globe in the pursuit of the peace, reconciliation, and openmindedness that Skali had in mind.

When I met Skali on a cold February morning at his hotel in New York City, he made a perfect first impression, a well-dressed, highly articulate, obviously gentle Arab. If there were a poster boy for the "good ones" in the minds of most Americans, Skali would be it.

Over coffee, Skali asked me to talk at the Colloquium about the idea of forgiveness. *Okay,* I thought, *I can do that,* although, in truth, I was a bit nervous about what I would say. I find that when the subject of forgiveness comes up, it's hard to find the place inside myself between overthinking what it means to forgive and trying to make everything seem like a giant Coca-Cola commercial where we all hold hands and sing "Kumbaya." But I was so excited at the prospect of participating in the festival that I figured I would deal with my queasiness later. After all, it was February and the Colloquium was not until June.

By April, I knew that it was time to start focusing on the lecture, so I tried to reach Skali to discuss my presentation. I wanted to know the questions that were central to him on the subject of forgiveness. I eventually received an e-mail from the Colloquium's staff, which said "forgiveness day" would examine Israel and Palestine, with the focus on how to avoid vengeance and practice forgiveness.

I groaned: it felt like a setup. Here I was, an American rabbi, traveling to a Muslim African country. What was expected of me? Was I supposed to stand up and explain how to solve the problems of Israel and Palestine? Was I supposed to present myself as a recovering right-wing fanatic, engaging in a public act of contrition? Did they imagine that I would say all the things they wanted to hear so that they could feel good about feeling bad about Israel? Their choice of this single topic in this particular location was itself problematic. There was no way such a supercharged issue could be confronted fairly in such a short time. I was also nervous because I wasn't told who else was to be on the panel with me, except that one was Christian and the other Muslim.

To err is human, to forgive divine popped into my head. Had the Colloquium been set up to contrast vengeance and forgiveness? Forgiveness, good; vengeance, bad? It was clear from the e-mails I received that the sponsors felt that evolved people, that is, those who wanted to create a peaceful world, would be committed to forgiveness, while anyone who was not ready to forgive was a vengeful evil person, contributing to the perpetuation of violence and war.

It was clear to me that in order to be useful at this event, I had to expand the axis between forgiveness and vengeance into something that was three-dimensional, reflecting the full spectrum of human needs. I did not know how to do that, but I knew that was the job.

Meanwhile, twenty people from CLAL had signed up to come with me to Morocco. Their part in the trip was vital to me. It made the difference between hopping on a plane and jetting off to one more talk, and sharing a journey with a wonderful group of people from a variety of religious backgrounds.

There were some small challenges along the way. My suit-case was lost en route. I couldn't believe it! I had specifically asked in New York if I needed to transfer my bag in Paris, and then checked in Paris to confirm that it was being placed on the plane to Fes. The answer was "no" to the former and "certainly" to the latter. But when I walked into the hotel to meet the group for the first time, I had nothing but a carry-on bag that contained my tallis and *tefillin*, a toothbrush, a sweatshirt, and a few notes I had brought with me to get ready for the talk. I did not have the books I needed; the clothing that would be appropriate (I was wearing a T-shirt and old hiking pants), or anything else. I couldn't even really wash up before meeting the group.

Usually these kinds of things don't bother me. But that afternoon in Fes, they did. I was tired, concerned about how to help the group come together, already a little nervous about balancing the Colloquium's desire to make everything nice with my own desire to make it more real.

When I walked into the seventeenth-century courtyard of the Riyahd Al Yacout, a restored urban palace in the heart of the Medina, none of my concerns mattered. Smiling faces and steaming mint tea greeted me. Everyone was happy that I had arrived and quick to remind me that I would not be the first person to wash out socks in the sink of a fancy hotel.

Our group's agenda was not limited to the Colloquium: the first night we were treated to an amazing performance by a group of Japanese percussion artists playing everything from chopsticks to drums the size of Volkswagens.

The second morning our plan included a walking tour of the ancient sites of Fes. A few members of the group didn't want to do all that walking and decided to check out the morning pro-gram at the Colloquium's Day of Forgiveness. When we met them back at the hotel for lunch, they were very excited, and not in a good way.

Two women from a group called the Circle of Bereaved Families had spoken. The first was Palestinian whose daughter had died in an Israeli military operation. Initially consumed by anger, she had come to realize that anger didn't help her deal with her daughter's death. It simply fed a rage that perpetuated her suffering. She said the only way she could begin to deal with the loss of her child was to forgive the people who had killed her. Hers was a beautiful story of letting go of anger, and the audience had been moved to tears.

Then an Israeli woman spoke. Her child had been killed in a Palestinian suicide bomber attack. She said there was no for-giveness in her heart, but only rage at the State of Israel, whose policies led young men to strap bombs on their bodies and blow themselves up. She said violence was the fruit of the seed of oppression, and the young man who had killed her daughter was himself a victim.

The same crowd that had been moved to tears by the Pales-tinian woman was now seething with rage at Israel, not exactly the hoped-for mood on this Day of Forgiveness. In fact the crowd was so out of control that the morning session had to be cut short, but not before the MC promised that that afternoon the audience would "hear from the rabbi."

I might as well go out and get a bucket of red paint, I thought, and paint a target on myself, because I was a dead man. What was I supposed to do? The morning session had broken apart because in their effort to focus exclusively on the healing power of forgiveness, which is profound, the organizers had ignored the anger in the room that was almost uniformly focused on Israel. They assumed that with the right words, people would simply forget their darker feelings. But those very feelings, because they were not addressed in an honest and evenhanded way, exploded instead.

That is always what happens when we ignore the full range of human responses to the biggest issues that we face. When we fail to acknowledge what is really going on inside ourselves, in our relationships, or in our world, because we are embarrassed by it or afraid that we can't deal with it, it ambushes us unexpectedly. By failing to include the need for justice alongside forgiveness, we actually make it harder to achieve either. Again I was reminded of the two lawyers and their arguments in Karin's murder trial. Again I found myself wrestling with how to integrate justice and forgiveness.

All too soon I was standing before about seven hundred people, only a smattering of them Jewish, knowing full well how much anger had been unleashed that morning. Half of you are waiting for the other half to apologize, I said. But the other half of this audience is waiting for the same thing from you! Everyone here who supports Israel wants the Palestinians and their supporters to apologize for the terror and death that has come in the name of creating a free Palestine. The exact same thing holds true for the Palestinians and their supporters, who are waiting for those who support Israel to beg forgiveness for years of oppression and cruelty. Everyone here has a decision to make. We can either stare at each other like gunfighters in a showdown at the OK Corral, each side waiting for the other side to apologize. Or we can admit that each of us is the person who both needs an apology and who owes one. I could tell that the audience was intrigued, although they still seemed a little suspicious. This has nothing to do with admitting moral equivalence or the historical accuracy of the other side's claims, I continued. This is about emotional equivalence and accepting the honesty with which each claim is made. Even if honestly held views are based on ignorance or delusion, they have to be addressed for at least three different reasons.

First is that such views define the beliefs, worldview, and frame of reference of the person or people whom I hope to engage. My telling you that something you believe in is wrong isn't going to help the conversation; you have to meet people where they are. Second, failing to meet them where they are demeans them in precisely the way we think they are demeaning us. If a person or group holds a view we find repugnant, they probably feel our views are repugnant as well. If we don't take them seriously, why should they take us seriously? You can't be someone else's teacher until you're willing to be their student. And, third, they may be right, at least partially. After all, if we are not prepared to consider that it is we who may be ignorant or deluded, our thinking is as closed as theirs. Our fear of moral equivalence first keeps us from appreciating the importance of emotional equivalence; it keeps us from understanding that, ultimately, we each want the same thing. We need to begin talking to each other. Without that conversation, people will keep on dying.

That got the crowd's attention. By shifting the discussion away from a moral calculus of right and wrong, without denying that those categories exist, I had succeeded in making space in the room. And I know that making space—sometimes intellectual, sometimes spiritual, and sometimes physical—for each other is the first step in addressing conflict.

We have been taught that good people are forgiving and bad people are vengeful, I continued. But I think we have to become more sophisticated in our thinking to appreciate the full range of responses to conflict. Rather than simply state that there are two options here—vengeance or forgiveness—we need to understand that our needs for justice and mercy are also part of who we are. They are all authentic responses, which address some part of our need to deal with past wrongs.

Isn't that how it works in life? Doesn't the drive for what I call justice sometimes translate into what others experience as revenge? Might not my attempt at mercy be seen as subverting justice? When does forgiveness become a dangerous form of forgetfulness? On the other hand, if we can never forgive, won't we be consigning ourselves to a life of bitterness?

Imagine setting up a new paradigm, one in which there are two axes, with revenge and forgiveness running along the horizontal, and justice and mercy running along the vertical.

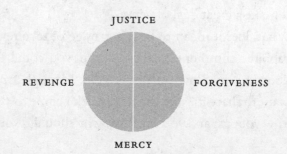

At each juncture of our lives, with every conflict that arises, we need to allow ourselves the full range of emotions, from the desire for vengeance to the readiness for forgiveness—and then ask ourselves what would be gained or lost by acting on each of those impulses.

Part of what makes us human is that we are not above taking revenge and bearing a grudge, and it's interesting that the Bible prohibits both of these things in chapter 19 of Leviticus. The Bible never prohibits things people aren't already doing. This prohibition in Leviticus directly precedes the directive to love one's neighbor as oneself. At first blush, this seems an odd juxtaposition of one of the Bible's most beautiful and affirming principles and a fundamental prohibition against what might be seen as our basest instincts.

What if those two directives are related? What if the reason I am able to get past my desire to nurture or avenge the memory of a past hurt flows from my awareness that in doing either of those things I am hurting myself? After all, the same verse that forbids grudges and vengeance teaches me that in loving you, I am loving myself. If I can't feel that level of connection between us, that loving you is like loving myself, then prohibiting me from either bearing a grudge or taking revenge doesn't make a great deal of sense.

What does it mean to bear a grudge or take revenge? Ancient rabbinic commentators say that if you come to me and ask to borrow my plow, and I say, "No, I love that plow and I don't want to share it," and the next week I come to you and ask to borrow your ax, and you say, "No, why should I, you wouldn't lend me your precious plow," that's revenge. If I reply, "Yes, even though you were a jerk when I asked you to do the same for me last week," that's bearing a grudge.

I think, by the way, that the examples used are seemingly so small because we are inclined toward these forms of behavior over even relatively insignificant things. Both bearing a grudge and wanting revenge are just responses, in the sense that any time we're not playing by the same rules, we shouldn't be obligated to each other. The basis of any just legal system—not to mention any healthy relationship—is that we should be treated equally. Without that expectation, why should we expect a reciprocal relationship?

I could justify my grudge by saying, "All I'm doing is trying to correct your bad behavior and teach you to act with more generosity in the future." Of course, this assumes that equality is of value even when it means treating each other equally badly, and that the best form of moral education is to make someone else suffer so that he will see the error of his ways. This is like hitting kids to get them to stop hitting their siblings. Every parent knows how well this approach works.

And yet that is what the quadrant of the marriage of justice and revenge is all about. You did something to me, which justifies my doing it to you. Or, even better, you did it to someone else who can't defend himself, so now I have the right to do it to you so that it will not happen again. That marriage of justice and revenge is always a death spiral. We know that all it does is give us just enough moral high ground to do to other people precisely what we wouldn't want done to us. Of course, it satisfies our visceral sense of fairness, but what good is that if it means that by treating each other in the same way, we are causing each other pain?

I watched this kind of tit-for-tat unfold one day at lunch in a New York deli with two friends. Sam made a deeply hurtful remark on the progress of Andy's career, something about his not having made partner at a firm where he had invested years of hard work and upon which he had pinned his hopes. Andy made light of the comment, but it was clear that the hurt had gone deep. A week later, Andy had the opportunity to strike back, and made a cutting remark at a party about Sam's difficult marriage.

If justice is simply about parity, then Andy was in the right. He had rebalanced the scales, which is a common way of understanding what justice is about. In this quadrant, revenge comes in on the coattails of justice. We know, however, that justice should be about something more than that. While the need to rebalance the scales is powerful—and necessary—there has to be a better way to do it. That is why Leviticus explores the link between justice and revenge, and why of all four quadrants in our new paradigm, that behavior of taking revenge in the name of justice is the only one that is completely forbidden by the sages.

Andy had been hurt, truly hurt. But in acting the way he did, he didn't heal that wound. None of us does when we behave that way, which we all seem to do at one time or another. You weren't home when you promised to be, we say to our spouses, so I'll be late next time. You weren't there for me emotionally, we say, so why should I worry about you now? We feel that we should do back to others what's been done to us. Isn't that the biblical command (also in Leviticus) of an eye for an eye? Actually, no.

In ancient times, when someone lost an eye or a limb, it was common to take both of the guilty party's eyes or limbs in retribution. Leviticus teaches *only* an eye for an eye—a radical limitation in its day on how people thought about justice and its limits that insists on basic human equality, even in the face of unequal behavior. It teaches us that justice is about more than vengeance.

Leviticus is often contrasted to the New Testament teaching about turning the other cheek, which is widely assumed to be a lesson in passivity. Not true. Jesus lived in Palestine when it was ruled by the Romans, for whom it was a sign of weakness to strike another person with the back of the hand. Yet that's precisely what happens if I turn my cheek when you and I are facing each other and you go to hit me, and you, like most people, are right-handed. You have to go past my left cheek and backhand me to get a good blow. In Roman times, that meant you were confronting your own weakness even as you exercised power over me. Jesus teaches us not to *ignore* the wrong done to us; he wants us to force those who would punish us to experience how they are diminished by their lack of mercy.

While we can't always forgive what has been done to us, we can marry our need for an aggressive response to our capacity for mercy. That capacity will not keep us from acting against someone who has hurt us, but it will cause us to act differently than if we indulge our impulse to marry justice with vengeance. The Bible illustrates this teaching in the Book of Numbers. Moses instructs the Israelites to build cities of refuge when they establish their new state in the land of Canaan. These cities will be places to which anyone guilty of committing an accidental homicide can go.

Suppose you're chopping wood and the ax head flies off and kills someone. Or you're driving toward an intersection and your brakes fail and you kill my wife, the crossing guard. There were six cities of refuge in the Holy Land where you could run and were untouchable. What do I mean by untouchable? Well, in ancient times (and often in not so ancient times), the close relatives of the victim were likely to want the killer's life in revenge. The Torah's response to that reality was these cities. The Bible never says we shouldn't *want* revenge: wanting it is normal! Instead it acknowledges that there is a real cost, even when something happens by accident. Indulging our inclination toward revenge is not such a good thing, however. The Bible tells us to be aware that while the urge for vengeance can be legitimate, acting on that urge is not.

If we could hold on to just that one insight, our national debate about the death penalty would be much healthier. As it is, we are polarized. On one side we have a group of people who cheer when the lights flicker outside the prison, and on the other a group who cries at the loss of another human life without having anything meaningful to say to the executed person's victims.

If we could hold on to that insight in our personal lives when we or someone close to us has been deeply hurt, we could respond in better ways, with something more than the choice between getting even (as if that were ever possible in the truest sense of the word) and getting down on ourselves for not being able to simply get over it. In both cases the key lies in our ability to merge the impulse toward revenge with the capacity for mercy. When that happens we build cities of refuge, sometimes in the world and sometimes in our own hearts.

While we can say very little about where these cities actually were in the Holy Land, or how life was organized in them, we know that the people consigned to them were instructed to "go there and live." No matter what has happened, the Bible wants life to continue, perhaps not exactly as before (how could it?). That's what the marriage of mercy and vengeance is all about.

Now let's look at our third quadrant—the overlap of justice and forgiveness. This may be my favorite of the pairings. Capital punishment is the classic case of justice meeting forgiveness in the Hebrew Bible.

You may well ask how capital punishment is linked to forgiveness. Aren't they antithetical? At first glance, so it would appear. Dozens of crimes warrant capital punishment in the Bible: murder, Sabbath violation, homosexuality, witchcraft, false prophecy, and adultery, to name just a few. Let's leave aside our feelings about the kinds of things that used to get you dead. If you think this list makes sense, great. If not, consider that future generations will look at the things we kill each other over and think them just as odd.

Even with all the biblical crimes that call for the death penalty, however, only once in the five books of Moses does a court execute a person for the violation of a law. In the Book of Numbers, Moses and Aaron stone to death a man who gathered sticks on the Sabbath. You may wonder why this is the exception. Despite thousands of years of commentary, this incident still remains shrouded in mystery, and I think that's the point: perhaps any time we really think we know someone has to die, they probably shouldn't have to.

How is it possible that so many things are seen as worthy of capital punishment, yet during all those years in the desert, with one exception, no one is executed? What if the point is to teach us precisely that? What if we need to learn that there are things that go on in this world that are so horrific that the person responsible for them really does deserve to die? What if the call for justice—the need to stand up and take sacred action with all our might for that which we believe—is important and necessary; and that is why we need strong laws on the books. But you know what? In practice we're rarely going to enforce them. Instead we're going to practice forgiveness because although in principle the perpetrator of the crime deserves to die, we're not going to kill anyone today. We acknowledge that there is a difference between claiming that someone deserves to die and taking it upon ourselves to carry out the sentence. The call for justice, even extreme justice, may be appropriate, but so is the recognition that those calling for it ought not to implement it more than a tiny fraction of the times they think that they should.

Nowhere is this view clearer than in the ancient rabbinic teaching about the death penalty. The rabbis insist that execution is an appropriate response, in principle, to a horrific crime; but they teach that any court that carries out that sentence even once in seven years is a terrorist court. In fact, in the Mishna in which this ruling is found, Rabbi Eliezer ben Azariah teaches that the death penalty must not be given even once in seventy years, and Rabbis Akiva and Tarfon teach that if it were up to them the death penalty would never be imposed at all. Amazingly, none of these rabbis ever call for the ruling to be erased from the books, or even make excuses for its presence! They understood that having the rule, even if it's never imposed, is an expression of power and principle, not weakness and muddy thinking.

If only we could bring this perspective to the death penalty debate. A man drags a woman from a car and rapes and kills her. To the people who say that man should die, I say you're right. The theory behind the death penalty is something I support. But justice is never pure. By the letter of the law you may be right, but there is a larger principle at work, one that recognizes that the questions of ultimate justice are better answered by whatever power we deem to have infinite understanding and wisdom. Unless you claim to be that authority yourself, then the demands of justice and forgiveness invite us to keep the death penalty on the books but almost never use it, if we use it at all.

In fact, the rabbis raise that sense of modesty to a sacred level in a radically surprising way when it comes to the death penalty. Unlike most legal systems, in which the toughest penalties are only imposed if the court is unanimous about imposing them, in Jewish law, if all rabbis agree, the death penalty cannot be imposed! Rather than seeing unanimity as a guarantor of justice, they see it as a sign of oversimplification and a good indicator of faulty reasoning. If, they argued, a full court of either twenty-three or seventy-one sages all comes to the same conclusion about something as complicated as a capital case, then something is wrong. The truth is never that simple or one-sided. Any

time we think it is, we should be extremely careful about what
actions we take in the name of that kind of truth. According to
the Mishna, that kind of truth is actually dangerous, while the
willingness to live with doubt is sacred.

Imagine what it must have been like in the rabbinic system
when they actually did execute someone in a rabbinic court.
The one thing of which all the judges were assured was that the
day following the execution, when they reconvened, as many as
half of the people sitting there believed that the other half were
murderers for killing an innocent man. And yet they came back
together to continue hearing cases. They accepted responsibility
for their own views and embraced each other as colleagues in a
shared pursuit at precisely the moment that they differed about
which policy would achieve their desired goal. That was what I
was asking of the audience that afternoon in Fes.

The last quadrant of our grid is the overlap of forgiveness
and mercy, the place inside us where we find the capacity
to experience the hurtful and painful things that have happened
in our lives as if they never really happened at all. This is more
than simply forgetting the past—more than some kind of spiritual amnesia. It allows us to move forward despite what has happened. It is about discovering a kind of forgiveness that is so
profound that it changes the present, redirects the future, and
revises the past. We each have to decide for ourselves when that
is the right quadrant for what's happening in our lives, but it can
be done and you don't need the patience of the Buddha or the
gentleness of Jesus to do it.

A wonderful example of how to accomplish this comes on Yom Kippur, the Day of Atonement, the holiest day of the year in the Jewish calendar. Jews all over the world recite the thirteen attributes of God's mercy, drawn from conversations between Moses and God when Moses wants to remind God how good God is so that God doesn't destroy the Jewish people for the sin of the golden calf.

But here's the great thing—the text that we recite on Yom Kippur is a lie. We cut off Moses' description of God in the middle of his words. We say God is merciful, gracious, and forgiving, and will wipe away all our past wrongdoing. In the same text, however, Moses describes a God who will keep track of our sins for generations, a seeming contradiction! What's going on?

The genius—the sacred audacity—of the authors of the Yom Kippur service is to amend what the Bible says. What chutzpah! How could they take such a liberty?

Deep down they knew that there was a truth that was bigger than accuracy, bigger than being right when we insist that the relationship between human beings or with God is so strong that we can get past anything—we can begin again. Some people call that atonement, being born again, or an experience of rebirth that comes with enlightenment. From the perspective of the framers of the Yom Kippur service, it's as if that nightmare in Sinai never happened—as if it were never there.

No one can demand that kind of leap from anyone else. But we've all wanted it, and my guess is that if it is something that we've all wanted, then it's something we should try to give to others as well.

The overlap of forgiveness and mercy is at the opposite end

of the spectrum from the overlap of justice and revenge. Instead of what I won't do for you because of what you wouldn't do for me, or what I am entitled to do to you because of what you did to me, here we have what I will do for you because of what I hope one day you will do for me in return, even if that never comes to pass. The indescribable power of this quadrant is that it is the only one of our four combinations that entirely depends on us, in which we can reside regardless of the actions of anyone else. The choice is totally ours.

We always have that choice in one form or another: we can choose to hurt back or convert our hurt to sensitivity to others. Yet inside each of us is the need for justice and vengeance, just as each of us needs forgiveness and mercy. It's not a matter of one or another of these needs being right and the other wrong. All are inextricably part of our experience, part of who we are, and the more we can honor and acknowledge all these facets of ourselves, the better off we'll be. I don't believe that to err is human and to forgive divine. All of our impulses have their place and whether we call them human or divine, all of them are sacred.

I was spent after my talk. I sat down to much applause, but the truth is, I had no idea which end was up. The tension of making these observations before this particular audience was suddenly acute. What had I done? Had I offended anyone? I really was not sure until two things happened.

I looked over to my left at Father Elias Kesrouani, a Lebanese-Palestinian priest, the chairman of the musicology department at Notre Dame University in Lebanon, and a presenter at the festival. I had met him as we were about to take the stage together. He was rail-thin, dressed all in black, with burning eyes and a manner that was as cold as ice. He greeted me as if I were a leper.

After my presentation, Kesrouani stared into my eyes with such intensity that I was rattled. What have I done, I thought! But then he reached over and took my left hand in his right one and raised it above both of our heads. That really got the crowd going. It's hard to describe the combination of joy and relief that I felt.

Kesrouani then made a fascinating remark. He said that there were many places where he differed from me in my analyses of particular texts, but that it didn't matter. The real issue was our willingness to live with genuine openness to each other's readings and our ability to see the sacred wisdom even in those with which we disagreed.

As I walked from the stage, Faouzi Skali, dressed as impeccably as ever, ran up and embraced me. "You are a Jewish Sufi!" he said. "You used your books to teach our *Wahdat*." I was gratified and moved and I began to look around to see if I could find the two women who had spoken in the morning session. I wanted to see what their responses were to the talk. But the hall had emptied, and I never was able to track them down.

CHAPTER FIVE

KEEPING SCORE

Making Judgments Without

Becoming Judgmental

I LEFT FES GENUINELY EXCITED ABOUT WHAT HAD HAPPENED. But I also found myself wondering about the implications of the encounter. Would it have any long-term effects? How would people integrate what they had experienced into their lives? When I wondered aloud about those kinds of questions with Barbara, a minister and academic from Oklahoma who had chosen to make this journey with me, she pounced on me.

"Bradley, why are you saying those things?" she replied in her Midwestern twang. "You need to have a little more faith— faith in your teaching and faith in your students!" Of course she was right. I was measuring people's insides based on my ability to see their outsides.

How often do we imagine that by finding a name for

something, we have understood it? We need words and labels in order to talk about each other, and about ourselves; but do those words ever fully capture the thoughts, feelings, and experiences about which we speak? Each of us could go on forever finding words for who we are. I think of the words that define me: man, Jew, white, American, husband, father, son, rabbi, friend. They are all one hundred percent true, yet none of them captures one hundred percent of who I am, and that would be the case no matter how long the list became. That's true for all of us. We measure each other and need categories to make each other recognizable, but at best they give us only a few facets of the diamond. There is no way we can see or comprehend all the facets, all the complexity, certainly not through one particular word or measure.

Maybe that's why God has so many different names in the Hebrew Bible: Adonai, Elohim, Shaddai, and on and on, to show that the label never fully captures the essence. Although one could argue that the single most important idea in Hebrew scripture is that there is "only" one God, we see God made visible under many different names. It's the same God, but that's the point. How could any God so big be understood with only one name?

The so-called polytheist traditions get a really bad rap from most monotheists. But, at their most sophisticated, it's not that polytheists think that there are many little gods. Instead, they know that whenever we talk about God, we are always talking about God as understood by us, so why not name all those understandings? Why not acknowledge the sacredness of

every manifestation of spiritual presence in the world? Why insist that there are a limited number of expressions of holiness.

The same variety, multiplicity, and complexity exist in human experience. Imagine if we would treat one another and
ourselves in light of this sense of mystery, an appreciation of
the profound complexity of each person's experience. It can be
hard, I know, to create the space in our hearts and minds to view
others in that way. How can we create that space? What im-
pedes us? What fills up the space where that openness, curiosity,
and receptivity want to be—no, *long* to be?

I first remember wrestling with those issues, in the context
of my own journey to make sense of prayer and the rituals that
surround it, in traditional Jewish practice when I went to the Ida
Crown Jewish Academy in Chicago. The Academy, as we called
it, was Chicago's coed orthodox Jewish high school, which combined a full day of regular high school subjects packed into the
hours of one to five-thirty in the afternoon after a morning of
Talmud, Bible, and Hebrew that began with prayers at eight.

This was not the kind of high school experience that my
parents had hoped for, especially as we lived in the district that
housed one of the finest public high schools in the nation, New
Trier. Film buffs will recall it as the school that Joel, played by
Tom Cruise, attended in *Risky Business*. In fact, I had to convince
my parents that it wasn't the right place for me by enduring a
semester at New Trier—the only student in its history to attend
classes in a *kippah* and *tzitzit,* a ritual undergarment, the fringes
of which hung conspicuously down below my shirt.

I may as well have hung a sign on myself that said, "Feel

free to mock this guy who clearly does not belong here." I did have friends. In fact, it was the first time in my life that I had good friends who were not Jewish. But I also had to confront students, usually very large seniors, who seemed to think that they were as obligated to pull off my *kippah* as I was to wear it. It wasn't fun, or a place in which I could study, pray, or live a normal life that happened to be orthodox. Ultimately my parents relented, and I transferred to the Academy.

Because I had struggled to enter the orthodox community, it was especially hard when its traditions didn't feel wise. In fact, I confess, I thought parts of orthodoxy stupid. One particularly pointless practice, it seemed to me, was the prohibition against counting people when you go to form a minyan (the minimum number of ten adult Jewish men required to be present for an orthodox religious service). Tradition, going back to the Middle Ages, tells you to pick a verse from the Bible with ten words and recite that to mark the presence of the ten men rather than looking at them and counting off. I felt this practice was contrived to say the least. Why not just count? Why words instead of numbers? It just seemed stupid! For this I was making my family crazy?

I went to one of my teachers, Rabbi Mayer Juzint, a tiny elf of a man. "What is this all about?" I asked. "Why words instead of numbers? Why can't we just count one, two, three, and so on?"

Rabbi Juzint had survived Auschwitz, and he had numbers tattooed on his arm. He could have looked at me and said, "You think this is a stupid tradition? Let me roll up my sleeve and tell you what happens when you start counting Jews or gypsies or gay people, or any people for that matter. I'm living proof of how dangerous it is when people become numbers."

Instead he simply explained that the tradition went back to the time of King David's unauthorized census of the Israelites. The story is recounted twice, once in II Samuel and again in Chronicles, and it's none too clear in either case. But the bottom line in each version is that in the final days of his rule, when his country was embroiled in civil unrest and competition over his successor, David wanted his subjects counted, and God said no. So, to this day, Jews do not count other Jews, since it would be like making a little census.

I was stunned by this explanation. It seemed arcane, even inane. This was the tradition that I had chosen? For this I had turned my family's life upside down? Rabbi Juzint's answer didn't help me at all.

The practice of not counting continued to look silly to me until years later, when I began to see the real damage that happens when we use demography instead of biography to understand each other. Demography, I saw, forced peoples' lives into preset categories. But good biography celebrates the richness and complexity of life. When we imagine that the best way to understand one another is by figuring out which category in our lives a person fits into, instead of asking how integrating that person into our lives will redefine the categories that we use, everyone suffers. We are using the scorecard we use in our own lives to keep track of someone else's score in life. I have caught myself doing just that with people who choose to remain single without children. I was raised in a loving family, and although some days I feel like running away to a cave, on balance I am convinced that replicating that experience is crucial to leading a happy, purposeful, fulfilling life. I have needed to learn that the exact opposite may be true for other people—that marital relationships get in the way for them of doing and giving and loving. We both want the same thing—love, community, connection—but we construct our lives in different ways. How often, however, do those of us with wives and children secretly or not so secretly feel that single people are lazy, self-centered, and selfish?

Although it may not be a big deal to count a group of people who have all gathered together for prayer, the idea that we should have practices that encourage us to see one another as unique individuals strikes me as incredibly wise. To be sure, common norms and standards upon which we can rely are important. Without them, we would find ourselves living in an entirely idiosyncratic, dysfunctional world. Religions are especially adept at creating a shared language and practice to help their adherents feel closely connected. But religions must always be on guard about the cost to those who don't embrace them or who embrace other religions. It is so easy to forget that the system that is right for you, even one that you believe God wants for you, may not be right for everyone. After all, how could the will of an infinite God ever be made so small as to fit into one finite system? Ironically, when it comes to our spiritual lives, we should be making the most room for one another, but it seems that instead we make the least.

When I became a rabbi, I began to see that the Jewish com-

munity was obsessed with numbers, with counting and catego-
rizing its members. Are they "religious" or "secular"? If they're
religious, what denomination are they? Are they "marginal" Jews
or "core" Jews (what is a marginal person anyway)?

Believe me, I appreciate that when you live in the generations immediately following the loss of six million members of
your family, it's natural to be obsessed with numbers and how
yours are holding. But I also know it's misguided when quantify-
ing a community—be it a religion, a nation, or even a family—
becomes the purpose of that community. When the existence of
the members becomes more important than their experience of
membership, something is wrong.

Does that mean that every pollster is a member of the SS
at Auschwitz? Of course not. But when we use the fixed categories of demography instead of the narratives that make up a
genuine biography to measure another person's spiritual experience or identity, we are in danger of moving away from creating
the kind of world we all want—where everyone matters, where
everyone has value and is appreciated for who he or she is.

The Bible can help us understand the innate, indelible
worth of every human being. The Bible says we are all made in
the image of God. Too often that is read as telling us something
about God and our own imperfect state. What if we read the
verse instead as a teaching about, first and foremost, who we are?
We are being told that each of us looks like God, not the usual
message that comes from most pulpits about God looking like
the individuals gathered in that particular house of worship. We
tend to want to make God in *our* image, to imagine a God who
looks, sounds, believes, decides, and acts as we act, or as we aspire

to act. But that's not God. That is *us* pretending to be God. In fact, each of us, in all of our diversity, reflects God's presence in the world. Until we appreciate that, we are doomed to keep beating up on ourselves and each other for not measuring up.

M y experience at the 92nd Street Y in Manhattan was a perfect example of how self-defeating it is to measure our internal spiritual journeys with external measures. It was an example of what happens when people keep score of their lives with other people's metrics and, worse, when we keep score of other people's spiritual lives with our own spiritual scorecards.

I was part of a colloquium titled "Are Jews Too Hip for Their Own Good." One of my fellow panelists was Sam Wolfson, the co-creator of *Jewtopia*, an off-Broadway comedy about a Gentile man who pretends to be a Jew online because he wants to find a Jewish wife. He meets and falls in love with a supposedly Jewish woman who ends up confessing that she's also a Jewish wannabe.

During our presentation, Sam, an incredibly energetic, creative guy, happened to mention his Asian girlfriend. He turned to me: "We gained two and we lost two," he immediately added with incredible guilt in his face and voice. It was obvious to everyone, myself included, that he was referring to the two Gentiles who converted to Judaism in *Jewtopia* (chalk up two for Judaism) and the fact that he was involved with a non-Jewish woman.

By his tally and the tally that I was supposed to be keeping as a rabbi (a transmitter and upholder of Judaism and someone who does not perform marriages between Jews and non-Jews, at that) I was supposed to be upset. But I wasn't. Or at least I was a lot more upset by Sam's pain than by the thought that he had found some happiness with someone who happened not to be Jewish.

In fact, that night was the first time I said out loud to a Jewish audience what I have felt for some time. If some genie offered me a contract that guaranteed that each of my three daughters would find the love of their lives and create loving, supportive, successful lifelong relationships with wonderful, intelligent, caring *Gentile* partners, I would sign in a heartbeat.

I admit that I want my girls to marry Jews, and I have created a life that makes it entirely more likely that they will—a life that is framed by values, practices, experiences, and ideas that flow out of three thousand years of Jewish life. I would like them to carry these values and practices because I believe that they contribute to living a more meaningful and ethical life. But I realize when I say I want them to marry Jews that it may not be the most evolved part of myself talking. It's a fine line between meaningful transmission and narcissistic replication when it comes to how we raise our kids.

My deepest desire is to be able to guarantee my children's happiness, not the Jewishness of the person with whom they find it. That had never been as clear to me as it was that night as Sam shared his scorecard for the Jewish people.

All his energy, vitality, and exuberance seemed to have drained from him as he made what he must have felt was his confession to me. He had bought into the idea that even though he clearly continued to feel deeply Jewish, he had failed himself and his people.

Whether he has or he hasn't shouldn't be a function of

who sleeps with whom. It should be a function rather of who and what he wants to be. If he wants to be with someone who isn't Jewish, how does he honor that relationship while still feeling that he is fully a part of the Jewish people? How does anyone do that?

What Sam was grappling with didn't even have to do with being Jewish. He was trying to integrate all the things that made his life wonderful, and the people he had been lucky enough to love, with the tradition in which he had been raised and about which he still cared enormously. How else is it possible to explain that he was sitting on a stage having this conversation with a rabbi, in one of the leading Jewish cultural centers in the most Jewish city in the world, with the possible exception of Jerusalem? How else could one explain that he had created a successful show about Judaism? If this is Jewish failure, bring on more!

This kind of challenge isn't confined to religion. How do James Carville, a committed Democrat, and Mary Matlin, a passionate Republican, stay married? They must have a bigger way of keeping score than partisan politics. They must appreciate that their ideological commitments, no matter how defining or important they may be, do not override the love and respect that they share; they are more important to each other than the ideas that divide them. When you make that leap, virtually anything is possible.

I was speechless for a moment after Sam's sheepish confession. His words were piercing, heartbreaking, expressing as they did the idea that somehow he—and we—had lost someone.

Sam had internalized the message that there are good Jews and bad Jews, and it is the bad Jews who go off with Asian women. The punishment? Banishment and exile and the message that you're a traitor to your people. Or, at the very least, that having committed this sin, it now must be corrected through his girlfriend's willingness to convert or at least commit to raising their as yet nonexistent children as Jews!

Every tradition has its internal barometer of goodness, its seal of approval. Each tradition has people who keep score and who like to say, "You're in, you're out." And Sam had counted himself out, internalizing the negative images that had been foisted on him. We really do see ourselves as others see us. If we are told we are lost or ugly, we take that on. It's no joke. By keeping score, we are creating each other. It is unrealistic to think that we can rise above or ignore how others think and feel about us and judge us. We're all deeply interdependent. We all want to be connected to each other. It's cruel when parents tell their kids to ignore taunts, when we recite to them the old adage about sticks and stones being the only things that can hurt us. What a lie!

How many people call themselves lapsed Catholics or bad Jews? Does that mean they no longer feel that those traditions are central to who they are? We tell people that if they don't meet our measure it's their problem, and sometimes that may be true; but it's a good idea for people doing the measuring to take a hard look at their rulers first. It always seems that their markers of success look suspiciously like themselves—and then we're back to making God look like us, rather than seeing how we all look like God.

People with life practices most like my own become very uncomfortable when I talk this way. They think I am legitimizing Sam's choices, authenticating them. But what does that mean? You are legitimate because you exist. To say, "I'll authenticate you" is the height of arrogance. We are all authentic. The word *authentic* comes from the Greek root *autos*: self. It doesn't come from the outside in, but moves from the inside out. At the end of the day, most of the measuring is about saying "How come you're not what I want you to be?" which pushes people to become unauthentic.

Does that mean every expression of the self is good? No. Does it mean that we should indulge every personal whim? Absolutely not. It just means that we will all have frustrations with people we love and the ideas to which we're committed.

People who are totally comfortable when I bash traditional standards of piety tense up when I say that to stop measuring other people doesn't mean we should stop measuring ourselves. Is who you are really who you want to be? No one can answer that question for you.

I try to be very careful about confusing my way of being spiritually connected and religiously committed with anyone else's way of doing so. In the end, that really is the lesson I took from my father's willingness to take me out for the shrimp that he believed were not kosher. He genuinely believed that not eating certain foods helped him to be a better Jew, but he could also appreciate that not everyone who cared about being Jewish did it that way.

Although my father was probably sitting at home in Palm Springs while I was at the 92nd Street Y, he was also with me on-stage as I explored with Sam the danger of keeping score. He was there giving me the strength to explain that while there are always limits and boundaries, we should never confuse ours with the only proper set. It was from him that I learned to strive to live my life with the awareness that other people's life choices and beliefs were equally valid and equally good.

My dad was there reminding me that while each of us has to make decisions and commitments, the ones that we choose for ourselves need not be the ones that others choose, and that disparate choices can each have integrity and value. The value of one decision's rightness need not be leveraged against the wrongness of all the others. Ironically, it may be leveraged against our ability to help others make the right decision for themselves and make sure that even if our decisions are different, we can continue to share the occasional dinner, regardless of what's on each other's plates. My father wouldn't eat ribs or shrimp at the restaurants we went to. But my mother loved them and so did his kids. He made a decision not to create divisiveness in his family. There is no doubt that my father had, in his mind, made a judgment and reached the conclusion not to eat pork or shell-fish because of his personal beliefs. But he also believed it wasn't right to coerce us to share those beliefs. What if we could treat our larger human family in this same way?

I encountered the worst kind of scorekeeping in the aftermath of 9/11. There were actually people in Jewish communities who took note of the disproportionate number of orthodox Jews who were not killed, relative to other Jews. *Are you kidding me?* I thought. I was angry, I was ashamed, I was horrified. I wanted to shake these people and say, "What are you talking about? That's the God you believe in? The God who decides who should live and who should die by counting up whether they waited this number of minutes or that number of minutes between milk and meat or lit candles on Friday night or went to the synagogue on the appropriate day?"

I believe with my whole heart that those are genuinely important questions. They can be the details in which both the proverbial devil and a hoped-for God are found. When details help us flesh out our values, when they are garments worn by our ideals, they are crucial. But when they become a goal in and of themselves, they twist those ideals into idols.

When people start imagining that how other people interpret religious practices are life-and-death issues, they are not so far from the people who flew the planes into the buildings. After all, if such decisions really are the stuff of life and death, then the murderers who piloted those planes were right to believe that how we live as Americans is a capital offense.

If failing to pray the "right" number of times a day, or deciding to eat the "wrong" kinds of food really are the things that bring one into whatever paradise or hell is imagined, then it makes sense to kill over those issues. If governments that place individual liberty ahead of religious ideology actually bring down eternal wrath upon the entire world, then it makes sense to kill a few thousand people in order to avoid that suffering for billions. We will differ only about which commandments God will kill us for breaking, and we will both believe that we understand the divine calculus according to which such things occur and be more than happy to share our wisdom with the rest of the world.

I also wanted to ask these people if they actually believed that the best way God has to communicate is to exterminate other human beings. Is that really how we are going to demonstrate the value of keeping kosher, by watching other people die because they failed to observe certain dietary laws?

This doesn't mean that I don't appreciate what people are doing when they try to figure out the cosmic justice of such horrific events. They are trying to keep from going mad, from giving up on the whole notion of such justice in a world that already appears to have done so. They are trying to hold on to a beautiful idea, in this case that a lifetime of commitment to a tradition that values life above all else will actually contribute to one's staying alive, in the face of overwhelming evidence against that belief. I would hope that we could find it in ourselves to have compassion for such people, no matter how infuriating they may be, because their own faith is hanging on by a thread, and that's really what they are trying to save. That doesn't mean we should go along with their theories, but a little compassion along with our judgments wouldn't kill us, either.

Plenty of people with no particular interest in religion or spirituality have told me that they believe God saved them on 9/11. Having gone through that experience, they have a right to make sense of it any way they can. Still, I find that response deeply troubling. Are they willing to sit in the living room of a young wife and mother who has lost her firefighter husband and comfort her by telling her that this is what God wanted? Are they ready to tell the parents that they buried their daughter, and not the other way around, because God willed it?

If we are willing to do that, then we have the right to talk about a God who saved us, and why we were saved. I have seen people who can do just that, a pastor comforting a family friend, for example, who had lost his brother. "Nothing happens without

God's will," the pastor said. "In the end, you will be comforted by your faith in that knowledge." For that pastor and that family, those were the right words. But not for me.

After all, by the reckoning of those people who thought more orthodox than non-orthodox Jews were saved that day, or those who believe that God saved them, we would have to insist that same God executed the other three thousand people who died in the towers on 9/11. Because if God did one, then God also did the other. We can't have it both ways.

The power to save is the same power as the power to kill. It doesn't work to invoke God when what you want happens, and then avoid God when what happens makes you sick, because at that point you are not really invoking God at all, you are invoking yourself and calling it God. Not that invoking God is always a bad thing. I remember sitting with a woman in the days after 9/11, a Catholic woman who had lost her mom in the South Tower. She said that she knew God had a plan, and much as she hated how it was playing out, she believed that it was for the best.

I don't know if there's a plan. I'm willing to admit that there is, or at least that I hope there is. But I am also willing to admit that I don't understand it. To pretend to understand God's plan is a dangerous thing. It's not God or religion or even the idea of a divine plan that is killing us. People who arrogantly assume that they can understand the full dimensions and meaning of God's plan are doing the killing.

How often do we justify things in the name of doing what God wants, or what our faith demands, or what the dignity of our religion, nation, or cause requires, regardless of the cost?

That's why I was in Hebron and that's why people murdered Jews for being in Hebron. That's why planes hit the Twin Towers and why the Crusades were fought. But however many points you may be scoring in the game you are playing, however much you think that some cosmic scorekeeper is made happy by how you play out your life, whether making sense of tragedies or finding your soul mate, it's important to remember that there are many ways to keep score, and even other games that could be played. The more important the game, the more important it is to remember that.

You may think I am trivializing by using the metaphor of a game to describe the painful and complicated issues with which many of us wrestle. But we all need to access simpler metaphors that, while not immune, resist complex exceptions and self-justifications.

For most of us, creating the space for other types of players and other types of games is easier said than done. It's hard for us to allow that there may be many different ways to keep score. The first time I really confronted my own beliefs about how we measure what counts as good and bad, as healthy or not healthy, was about ten years ago when I was directing a training program on how to work across denominational lines for rabbinic students from all the different denominations in American Jewish life. Our conversation turned one day to tattoos in Jewish tradition, probably because tattoos were becoming enormously popular with people other than marines and circus performers, and these future rabbis wanted to think together about how to respond to this trend, given the ancient prohibition against them.

Leviticus 18:28 prohibits making markings in one's flesh, which are understood to mean tattoos. There is a common, though false, assumption that people cannot be buried in a Jewish cemetery if they have a tattoo. Some of my students argued that the tattoos of biblical times were different from tattoos today, so perhaps the prohibitions of traditional Jewish law did not apply. Others declared that they didn't think of Judaism as a legal system that governed their daily existence, at least not at the level of ritual and lifestyle, so it didn't matter what Leviticus said.

That's all well and good, I said, but I am interested in how you respond to a tattooed Jew. Does it matter if the tattoo has a Jewish theme or image? How about the circumstances under which it was acquired? Or what motivated it? Does it matter that sixty years ago tattoos were markers for death for millions of people in Europe?

At this point a student named Sara, who had thus far not uttered a word, spoke up. She had read a story in *Ms.* magazine that she thought would be relevant to our conversation. A young woman had called her mother to ask which she found least objectionable, body piercing, ritual scarification, or tattoos. The mother hated them all, but found tattooing the least objectionable. In that case, the daughter said, would her mother please ask their rabbi how to write the word *survivor* in Hebrew. The daughter, a survivor of childhood sexual abuse, had suffered from extreme depression for years and had recently been released from the hospital following her third and most serious suicide attempt.

Having come to the conclusion that she really wanted to live, and having had a great deal of time to reflect on the scars that now ran up and down her arms from her suicide attempts, she had decided that she would tattoo "survivor" across those scars so that the next time she thought about taking her own life, she would be reminded that she really wanted to live and that she could survive anything. Sara said that the daughter wanted the word in Hebrew because for her that solidified the sacredness of her commitment.

We were all silent.

"How should we score that?" Sara asked.

None of us quite knew, but we all had been given a lesson in how difficult it can be to keep score for other people. I had been trained to explain as meaningfully and intelligently as I could that tattoos are forbidden—period. My job as an upholder of my tradition was to persuade people to honor the rules as "we" understood them. There was no distinction made between our understanding and the right understanding, nothing that prepared me for a story in which something that was forbidden in general became holy when incorporated into the life of a particular person with a particular set of experiences. And, truthfully, that's how most of us are about most things in life: the more certain we become about something being right, so right that it shapes our lives and how we are, the more we seem to forget that it might not be right for others.

After Sara's story, I knew in no uncertain terms that not all tattoos were created equal, that the choice was not between upholding an ancient tradition and undermining its authority, but in appreciating the way every practice is different, even if it looks the same from the outside, because every practitioner is different.

What a tattoo means when it is a marker for life really is different from what it means when it is a marker for death. That was the case in the concentration camps as well as in Leviticus (because it was associated with ancient pagan death cults). I still honor the prohibition against tattoos, even though I think that they are beautiful and would love to get one, especially a symbol of unity or wholeness that comes from some other tradition or culture, one that would demonstrate that the values I hold as deeply Jewish are held by others as deeply Buddhist, Native American, or Christian—that would demonstrate that although those values are claimed by many traditions, that does not make them any less central to whatever tradition each of us claims most specifically.

I have come to accept that what is forbidden to me may be a sacred practice to someone else, and for the exact same reasons. That's why I don't use the word *outreach* in any of my work. The word for outreach in Hebrew, *kiruv,* means to bring close. The underlying premise is that other human beings are far away. Far from what? From themselves? That's not possible, unless they are mentally ill, in which case they need a therapist, not a rabbi.

Words like *kiruv* and *outreach* imply that people are far from our understanding of whatever it is we're trying to teach them, and that they would be far better off if they simply lived or thought as we do. But that's not spiritual growth, that's narcissism. Spiritual growth occurs when you become not more like your teachers, but more like the person that you most want to be, by using the lessons that your teachers provide.

There is something to learn from communities that are constantly keeping score of their members. When I was a student in the yeshiva, there was enormous competition to see who could put in the longest hours in the study hall. Did that create lots of unhealthy pressure? Sure. It also helped me to discover intellectual stamina that I never knew I had and would not have discovered had I not been living in a community of people interested in keeping score for me.

There is no life without accountability. Among traditional religious communities or those in any tradition possessing fierce faith, be it political, scientific, or spiritual, there are always fierce scorekeepers, and there is wisdom in that. But that doesn't mean we need to be unsophisticated, unforgiving, or unloving about how we keep score. The issue is not whether or not we keep score, but how and for whom.

To the extent that there is a practice connected to these things, it is putting the words "for me" at the end of any claims we make about living in the best country or religion—or relationship, for that matter. It's okay to make passionate arguments for why we've reached the conclusion of what's right for who we are. Putting "for me" doesn't mean dulling our passion. We need all the passion of the world's scorekeepers with the discipline to set limits on how far those passions extend. We need real discipline that sets standards about how many hours we will study, or how many times we will have the same conversation with our kids, or how much money we will share with people who have less than we do, and those standards need to be upheld. But it takes even more discipline to live with those standards while recognizing that what's true for me need not be true for you.

I think it's okay to say what is right or wrong and keep score inside a particular group. It's okay to say that we really think intermarriage is a bad idea for us—as long as we don't apply that standard to everyone. Sam wasn't hurt by knowing that many people are opposed to Jews marrying non-Jews; he was hurt by the absence of an alternative view.

In fact, if your limits don't have limits, you're not a limit-setter at all. If your limits don't have limits, you are as out of control as the people you accuse of being without discipline.

We all make judgments. What's important is not to let those judgments get in the way of making room for the parts of a person we don't understand and appreciate. What's important is to preserve our capacity to make judgments without becoming judgmental.

My father said that if we pointed a thumb at ourselves every time we wanted to point an accusatory finger at someone else, we would all be a lot better off. Most religious traditions point fingers at other people instead of pointing thumbs at themselves. Religions should make people feel safe enough to be able to point a thumb back at themselves. Pointing a thumb never fails!

In Sam's story we see the hurtful, damaging side of scorekeeping in which we learn to count ourselves out. In the 9/11 story we see the awful side of the thinking that counts others out. It's one thing to feel you understand God's plan for you and another to say you understand God's plan for someone else.

Keeping score is important. Measuring ourselves and taking stock of our lives is important; where we're going and where we want to be are really important questions to ask. But please remember that the best score we keep is our own.

CHAPTER SIX

MOSQUECHURCHAGOGUE

Finding Unity, Not Forcing Uniformity

"MY HOUSE WILL BE A HOUSE OF PRAYER FOR ALL PEOPLES," says the prophet Isaiah in his vision of what the world will be like after the Messiah comes. The beauty and wisdom of this vision has nothing to do with whether or not you believe in Isaiah, the Messiah, or God. Most of us have imagined a perfect world, or at least a world less blighted by poverty, disease, and bloodshed than the one we now inhabit.

Isaiah's prophetic vision of a perfect world rests on the principle that "perfect" looks different to different people. Isaiah's house of prayer is for all *peoples*—plural, not singular. It most emphatically does not require a flattening-out of all distinctions. It is not a world in which everyone shares the same set of beliefs, and all differences have been erased and all bumps smoothed. It is not a world in which everyone who disagrees with me will eventually think the way I think and believe what I believe.

Isaiah's prophetic vision is far more ambitious—and attainable! It envisions unity without demanding uniformity. His house of prayer is a place where we will all be able to stand under one roof with our differences on display. We won't need to check any part of who we are at the door in order to get in, whether we're a "born again" Christian, Hasid, Shiite, Sunni, Republican, or Democrat.

Too often we are made to feel that we're being asked to hide or leave behind pieces of ourselves that we're afraid other people may find disagreeable. Isaiah says no. Bring it all. Bring all of who you are. Bring all those things that make you you!

Can you imagine this prayer house? Imagine an actual physical space for all nations to come together, and a space within that house or place for each of them, with all their differences in customs, beliefs, language, dress? I'm not talking about something like the UN, at least not as it's currently constructed because it is a place of negotiation, which means that it functions as I do when I step in and negotiate a truce between my kids. None of them is fully happy with what I impose, but they can live with it. Isaiah's house of prayer, on the other hand, is not a place of negotiation and compromise. It's a place where we would stand shoulder to shoulder and recite all of our different prayers from all of our different religions in all our different tongues because any God big enough to pray to is big enough to hear every language and form of prayer.

I first had a glimpse of Isaiah's vision when I was in Hebron—but I was too young and pigheaded to see it. Hebron *is* Isaiah's house for all peoples—or at least it *almost* is—in the way that I have been told by biologists that orangutans and humans are almost the same chromosomally (What a difference that one percent makes!). Hebron was a sacred Jewish burial ground, the resting place of Abraham and Sarah and their progeny. After the rise of Islam, Muslims took control of the city, and a mosque was built above the cave for Abraham. According to both the Koran and the Hebrew Bible, Abraham was the father of Ishmael, so this site was also a holy place for Muslims. During the Crusades, Christians poured into the Holy Land and wrested control of sacred sites from the Muslims. The Christians, who also claimed Abraham and Sarah and their children as part of their sacred tradition, turned the mosque into a church. As power shifted back and forth between Muslims and Christians, the site was alternately church and mosque. During the Ottoman Empire, it became solely a mosque again, and stayed that way until 1967, when the State of Israel took control of Hebron. Shortly thereafter a synagogue was established inside the mosque, and I went there to pray in 1981 under the Israeli army's protection on Shabbat.

I have come to think of this place as a *mosquechurchagogue,* a site that could have been—and still could be—Isaiah's house of prayer for all nations. The building above the tomb of the forebears of our Western religious traditions could truly integrate the sacred stories from Judaism, Christianity, and Islam. Instead, of course, that place has come to represent hatred and intolerance. The different sides who battle over it are stuck in a way of thinking and feeling that insists that the only way to prove that what is mine is really mine is to make sure that it's really not yours.

Why is it that to make things, even spiritual things, more ours, we so often have to make them less someone else's? Why does being right depend on everyone else being wrong? Do other children need to be failures in order for ours to be successful? Do other women need to be ugly in order for my wife to be beautiful? In love and beauty we can make room for difference, or at least we seem to know that we should, but we have a harder time applying this expansiveness to tradition and truth.

Ironically, the so-called secular politicians in Jerusalem who established the policies that guided our use of the Makhpelah, politicians who probably couldn't even quote the verse from Isaiah, had a better understanding of his messianic vision than do most supposedly religious Jews and Muslims who spend their lives studying sacred books. In setting policy for the use of the mosquechurchagogue of Hebron, these secular politicians worked to ensure that all people who wanted access to that place could have it, regardless of their faith or ethnicity. They didn't try to get everyone in there at the same time—that would have been too much to ask. But they did appreciate, even as they established settlements and proclaimed that Hebron was going to remain under Israeli sovereignty, that the Makhpelah could be simultaneously holy to both Jews and Muslims.

Their view was the polar opposite of that espoused by

their religious counterparts. During the second intifada, which broke out subsequent to Ariel Sharon's visit to the Temple Mount, the Mufti of Al Aqsa, the spiritual leader and institutional head of the third-holiest and most potentially explosive religious site in the Islamic world, and the chief rabbi of Israel made public declarations about the impropriety of the other community's claims to the site. The Mufti insisted that there had never been a Jewish Temple in Jerusalem, let alone two of them, and that the site was purely Muslim and always had been. Israel's chief rabbi responded that there was no Muslim claim to the site because from the seven layers of the world, which reach below the surface of the earth, to the seventh layer of heaven, the Temple Mount was uniquely and exclusively Jewish!

They agreed with each other about the real issue, which had nothing to do with either the place or its history. Each side believed that the only way it could fully claim its connection to the Temple Mount was to eliminate the other's claim. They agreed that for something to be theirs, it must be theirs *exclusively*. Imagine if we treated our children that way. Or our friends. Actually, we too often do, and when we do, it's never pretty.

It was the secular politicians who insisted on the right of all groups to have access to the site. This is yet another instance of secularists acting in a way that is more religious than people do who are traditionally observant. But because they couldn't (or didn't) articulate the spiritual dimension of their position— in this case, liberal democracy—it made it very easy for people like me to disregard the spiritual validity of their politics. I would have perked my ears if they had said that in the name of the Bible and its highest ethics, in the name of Isaiah's prayer house for all peoples, we will ensure that *everyone* will be guaranteed full access to holy places. Sacredness is *not* a scarce commodity. We betray our faith and the essence of our aspirations for thousands of years by being stingy.

One small incident in Hebron has come to represent for me the way I sabotaged Isaiah's vision. Each Saturday we had services in the synagogue inside the mosque—tense sessions of worship because the Palestinians hated it that we were there, celebrating our control of the space. We, of course, hated it that they were around, too.

We finished Saturday services with a *Kiddush*, serving food and saying a prayer over wine. According to the Israeli government at the time, wine could not be brought into the synagogue because it was also a mosque, and alcohol in a mosque is a gross violation of Muslim faith—which made it even more delicious to smuggle it in. At the end of the day, when you weigh your country's rules against God's rules, God wins.

To avoid getting caught, we would pour the wine into the kids' canteens, which the guards and soldiers didn't check. Never mind that we were giving the finger to the Muslim faith. We knew that we were right and they were wrong. This place was ours, not theirs. End of story.

It wasn't just the Palestinians we were dissing. One of the building's guards was an observant Jew. He was *one of us,* but no one gave a damn about the problems our alcohol caused him. No one cared that as citizens of the state we had to respect its laws, even if we didn't agree with them. No one cared that in the name of our politics and our way of understanding Shabbat, we made *his* Shabbat worse—not only by keeping him from his home and family, but by making his job much harder than it had to be.

That was a clue that something was wrong, but I wasn't paying attention and neither was anyone else in our group. Forget that we had no respect for other people; we had no respect for our own. The circle had become so tight that anyone who was willing to enforce rules that differed in any way from ours, even if he was one of us, was cut out. That's the way being right works. First you exclude everyone who isn't a member of your religion or nation. Then it's everyone in your nation or religion who doesn't agree with you. And then it's everyone who only "sort of" agrees with you. And pretty soon it's down to you and me, and frankly I have my doubts about you.

The army stopped us as soon as they saw what was happening. And, you know, it didn't matter! We had brought the wine in just to prove a point. You can say the same prayer over grape juice. In our way of thinking, however, our rules had to be the only rules. We couldn't be fully present until the Palestinians were fully absent.

It has been said that the opposite of truth is not a lie but a bigger truth. Truth is not found by falsifying everything else. When we do that, we are trying to make truth small, an irreducible essence. But truth is an additive process. It is bigger than any single space we inhabit.

That does not mean I don't believe in truth with a capital *T*, or that I'm a relativist. I'm not. I don't find myself paralyzed by the idea that it really might be okay for people to blow up buildings filled with innocent people "in order to make the world better," or for adults to have sex with children to "initiate them into their own sexuality," or for people to shoot physicians who perform abortion because "that is what God demands." I am willing to fight against those things. I believe in truth with a capital *T*. But truth has to be bigger than any one time or place. It has to be more than a firmly stated commitment to those things in which we already believe. It has to be so big that it demands modesty and constant reevaluation on our parts.

The relativist cannot act, because he believes that no one can say what is right and what is wrong. That is tragic. The absolutist is always acting because the truth is already fully known and is simply waiting for its adherents to make it real, no matter what anybody else thinks. There is a truth in Mahatma Gandhi telling his followers not to fight back if a British soldier fired at them. And there is truth in sending young men like my father to fight in a world war alongside those same British soldiers. We need more practices in which one of those truths holds on to the other as a corrective. If Dr. King and Malcolm X had each found a way to honor each other's teachings earlier, for example, both might still be alive and America would certainly be a better place for all of us. Each would have seen the wisdom in the other's work, in the other's message, and found a way to support the wisdom that came from each approach. They could have shown us how to combine the truth of Malcolm's insistence upon self-reliance, independence, and communal self-empowerment with Dr. King's truth of the interdependence of all human beings and the importance of a shared human community that extends beyond a given race or faith. Perhaps that coalition would have proven too powerful for their assassins. Even if it had not, it would have shown our country a path that integrated two sets of needs all of us have: the need to assert ourselves and the need to find connection with others.

Here's another example of two competing truths. There's truth to the gay person's experience of opening the Bible and reading, near the beginning of the Book of Genesis, God's words, "It is not good for man to be alone." The Bible is telling us that loneliness, for most of us at least, is an unacceptable state. We could go even further and say the Bible is telling us that loneliness is a sin. It violates the story's fundamental understanding of what it means to be human, even to be a man. We are created to be in relationship, and that fact is taught before there's any discussion of whom we are to be in relationship with. The need for relationship is so fundamental that it supersedes all else. Before we knew that Leviticus believed it was a sin for a man to enter into a sexual relationship with another man, we learned that it was a sin to be lonely, so big a sin that God reordered creation to overcome it.

If loneliness is a sin, how can some of my fellow rabbis (and priests, imams, and other clergy, for that matter) tell a gay man who is in a loving relationship with another man that what he's doing is wrong? Well, they can, and often do, point to Leviticus, where homosexuality is prohibited. The Leviticus prohibition is based on the truth that the ideal state of human relations is for people of different sexes to come together and build families. Leviticus is very clear about telling us how life should be lived so that we maintain order and things fit together in their right and expected places.

Leviticus is also concerned about the ways in which people coming together will lead to the possibility of their making more people. It is more concerned with the role that people play in being like God (creating human life), while the Genesis story is focused less on being like God and more on feeling like God (having a new creation to keep from being lonely). Leviticus plays out the possibility that we humans can act like God in creating new life and organizing it on the planet. Genesis seems more interested, at that moment anyhow, in our ability to feel like God, to look around and sense the incompleteness of things and yearn for someone with which to connect. God made Adam and then realized that Adam needed Eve. It may also be why the notion of the Sabbath is so important to that story. We are told about God resting on the seventh day, precisely because we, too, need rest and to learn that to enjoy that rest is to also be like God.

Leviticus understands sacredness as a function of things being in their rightful places, not of how individual people feel about where things are being placed. It's the difference between the classically trained French chef, for whom everything must be done according to plan because following that plan assures the best product, and the short-order cook who knows that as long as the customers are happy, it really doesn't matter if everything was done according to what she learned at cooking school.

While it's easy to be impressed with the chef, most people are more at ease with the cook because they know that in his own way he is genuinely concerned with making a meal that is right for them. The chef can always hide behind rules, even if the customer hates the food. After all, he will reason, it's been prepared according to the rules, so it must be the customer's problem. As someone who loves to eat, I know that we need both the cook and the chef, and I suspect that's also true of the insights of Genesis and Leviticus.

Some people will say that using Genesis to justify homosexuality is obscene, while others despise the so-called truth of Leviticus. But, like the two cooks, each possesses wisdom. Liberal friends berate me because I don't perform same-sex marriage ceremonies, or those between Jews and non-Jews. Each morning I ask what is demanded of me in light of the traditions that I hold most dear, and the answer for me on whether to perform same-sex marriage or intermarriage ceremonies is no. I fully understand that it's one of those things for which, if there is a God that I have to stand before when I am dead and account for my life, I may get my head smacked and be told that I was a shmuck for not being more imaginative.

I have the luxury of having colleagues who do perform same-sex marriage and intermarriage ceremonies. Perhaps if I didn't I would be moved to take a different position. I'm not the only option. Still, I catch a lot of flak. But, of course, so do those who perform those kinds of marriages. Perhaps we need to stop pretending that there are positions that will satisfy everyone and get used to simply doing our best while admitting the price of the position that we have taken.

A final word on the alternative truths of gay marriage: In the Midrash, the rabbis imagine that after God says that it is not good for man to be alone, God brings the animals to Adam, and Adam makes love to each to see if any of them are, in the rabbis' words, "a proper fit." It is only after each proves to be not quite right that God makes something new—a woman.

And there's the rub. A gay man may say, "I don't care what you think of me, my good fit is a man." People may argue that the Genesis prohibition against loneliness trumps the Leviticus prohibition against homosexuality. Perhaps it's impossible to fully honor both of those truths simultaneously. The position that marriage should be between a man and woman should not be dismissed as narrow and small-minded. That's how marriage has been defined for a very long time, and it took thousands of years for that to become the norm in the Western world. When it did, it was considered a real upgrade from one man with many wives, or one man with one wife and many slaves with whom he slept (although I know few men who have not found themselves wondering about the possibilities of such traditions). We shouldn't expect to develop a new consensus overnight. Perhaps a new understanding of marriage should include polygamy! After all, if we're pushing for the acceptance of any mutually consenting arrangement, then why not include legal union between multiple partners? I may not favor that move, but I would love to see us recognize that each move we make has a cost, and to be honest about who is paying it and why.

What if we actually had the courage to make a commitment without being certain we were right? We are back to Abraham and his journey. What if we had the courage to set out on our journey without being certain of exactly where we were going? What if we knew the rough trajectory of our journey toward a better world, but we were not absolutely certain about the contours of that world?

While that question began thousands of years ago, it continues in this very moment. The various sides in our nation's debate about new kinds of relationships, families, and just about everything else, all claim that their position is motivated by their desire to bring about a better world. Like the Mufti of Al Aksa and the chief rabbi of Jerusalem, the warring sides actually agree about the most important thing: their shared motive. If our debates reinforced what we share, instead of our conflicting positions, we would shift from a culture of crusading pilgrims who view their opposition as infidels, to a culture of Abraham's children sharing a sacred journey. We would continue to have real disagreements, but those disagreements might not so often devolve into denigration. We should cherish our disagreements and differences, our lack of uniformity. The track records of societies that insisted on uniformity, from Mao to Mussolini, had little of which to be proud. Let's face it, final solutions are not the answer.

Both sides need to admit this—in all the divisive issues that make up our public life these days, whether we're talking about gay marriage, abortion, or gun control. I would love to hear gay rights activists say, in their push for gay marriage, "We may be making a colossal mistake." And I'd like to hear the same admission from the opponents of gay marriage. That admission on *both* sides is a prescription for the civility and thoughtfulness that is now so conspicuously absent from public life.

I lost my chance to embrace a mosquechurchagogue, Isaiah's house of prayer for all peoples, in Hebron. But I recaptured some of Isaiah's vision unexpectedly when I was finally ready to move toward a world in which we would all stand shoulder to shoulder, praying in our different tongues and creating previously unheard harmonies—a new music of the spheres.

I had been invited to visit the Islamic Society of North America, the largest Muslim organization in this country, at its headquarters in Plainfield, Indiana, a short drive outside Indianapolis. Thirty thousand people attend their annual meeting, where Iran's former president, Mohammad Khatami, spoke when he visited the United States. I appreciate that for some people that would have been reason enough to stay away, but if you want to reach someone, you have to reach them where they are.

That lesson is also part of the Abraham story. Ishmael, Abraham's first child and the world's first Muslim, and his mother Hagar find themselves cast out of Abraham's family. They are sitting in the harsh Judean desert, ready to give up on life itself, when God reaches out to them "where they are." If the biblical story can imagine that God is ready to reach out to Ishamel where he is, how can we do less? Especially in the name of faith?

My trip to Plainfield had nothing to do with endorsing Iran, its current president, Mahmoud Ahmadinejad, or its former one. I had been invited to speak at ISNA's Islamic Leadership

Development Center on Jewish perspectives on interreligious encounters and the spiritual imperative of establishing an intercultural conversation. In truth, I was probably trying to prove to both my hosts and myself that they had not made a colossal error in taking the unprecedented step of inviting a rabbi to address this gathering. I didn't want to give them interfaith pablum, what a minister friend of mine bitingly refers to as a happy hands-across-the-water moment, but I did want to help heal the hurt between our two faiths.

The day before the lecture, I met with Dr. Syed Syeed, a lovely man with a gleaming smile and a beautiful mane of white hair, who heads the organization and had also been its founder when he had been a doctoral student in engineering at the University of Indiana.

I had come to Plainfield with a colleague, Dr. Michael Gottesegen, in part to open up dialogue between ISNA and CLAL on how to bring Jews and Muslims together, a goal we both thought might be more readily achieved in America than in the Middle East, where the two sides were shooting rockets at each other. It's not that such efforts do not exist, but they are usually encounters between secularists who identify themselves as Jewish or Muslim, but have no real interest in examining the religious roots that fuel their problems. We were there to build relationships with people who are as proud of their heritage as we are of ours, and to see if those who are proudest could reach across the boundaries that divide us.

Michael and I sat in Dr. Syeed's office, which was lined with books and a few lithographs of verses from the Koran. As a religiously observant Muslim, Syeed avoided representational art, which, according to Islamic tradition, is a form of idolatry, the making of images that should be made only by the Creator.

Dr. Syeed and I chatted, getting to know each other, beginning to build a relationship. We were keenly aware that we represented communities that were often at each other's throats. They treated me with great deference, as though I were a visiting holy man, and I got the sense, which was both touching and ironic, that they had a deep admiration for the dazzlingly successful émigré experience of the American Jewish community and wanted to learn what they could from us in the hopes that they would be able, as a group, to emulate it.

Allahu Akbar. Allahu Akbar. The call for afternoon prayer rang out on the building's PA system. Devout Muslims pray five times a day, and both Syeed and Mohammed El-Sanousi, a Somalian and ISNA's director of public affairs, who had joined our meeting, rose.

I was faced with a decision. Should I follow them to the mosque? And do what? Watch them pray as if they were exotic animals in a zoo? On the other hand, I felt that if I remained in the office, I would be creating distance between two men who were quickly becoming friends. So I followed Syeed and El-Sanousi through their cavernous building toward I knew not what.

We walked down long corridors and flights of stairs and stepped inside a larger foyer with cubbyholes for shoes. The prayer room was enormous and could easily have held two thousand people. Off to the side was a washroom. Men performed ritual ablutions, and I noticed that El-Sanousi did a more thorough and aggressive job scrubbing and rinsing than did many of the other men. He not only washed his hands as the others did, but scrubbed his arms, legs, and feet, and he washed out his mouth. I wondered at the power the use of so much water must imply for someone from a drought-ridden country like Somalia. It seemed to me that his washing was not only a preparation for prayer, but a prayer itself, an offering of a scarce resource to show how serious he was about sharing himself with Allah. Perhaps because I was moved by that, I began to wash my hands as well, thinking that washing hands before prayer is a practice among many traditional Jews. I realized, if only unconsciously, that I was preparing myself to be not only a spectator but a participant in the ritual that was coming, although I still had no idea what that would entail.

Of course, I still didn't know what I was going to do as our two hosts, and the entire ISNA staff, finished washing and walked in stocking feet onto thick, cream-colored carpet. Michael and I had deduced that the folding chairs in the entryway were for visitors who didn't want to proceed into the mosque itself to pray, and Michael was looking at me, wondering what to do.

The huge open prayer room was completely devoid of images on its walls. Aside from a raised speaker's chair, which served as a small pulpit, and a few rugs placed at the room's front, the décor managed to be both luxurious and minimal. It was different from Hebron or any other mosque that I had entered. This was America. I was poised on the threshold, but of what I wasn't sure.

I would be lying if I told you that I thought about what was coming next. I stepped onto the carpet behind Syeed and followed him into the middle of the room, thinking how wonderful it would be as my toes felt the luxury of the pile if I could get my family to take off their shoes and our home could be carpeted like this.

As he and the others proceeded to the front of the room and fanned out in a single row, each of them wanting to be as close to Mecca as possible, I joined the line. After all, what actual prohibition could there be against doing that, I thought to myself. Then they called out the beginning of the service and dropped to their knees. And so did I.

I was not violating anything sacred to me by allowing myself to fall into a prayer pose in a room full of people who call God by virtually the same name that I do. God is Allah to them and Elohim to me—it's the same word! The spirit of Isaiah's prophecy was with me, and I began to realize that this experience in Plainfield was a shot at creating his long-predicted mosquechurchagogue, if only for a few minutes and if only for myself. It was a redemptive act for me.

As Muhammad, Syeed, and the rest of the men in the room recited the afternoon prayer, I did the same, except that my words were in Hebrew from the Jewish tradition, where we also have a short afternoon prayer. It begins with the words from Psalm 140, "Happy are those who dwell in your house," and continues with Psalm 145, an acrostic poem that enumerates all the things for which one can be grateful and happy. Not a bad practice to have for any of us caught up in the things that annoy or disappoint us during the course of a busy day. It's powerful to put those disturbances aside, without pretending that those troubles are not real or that a few mumbled words will simply make them disappear. Rather, the ritual asks us to focus on those things about which we can actually be happy in our lives.

It's not always easy to have a long list of such things, but at least one or two usually come to mind. By taking the time to recall those one or two causes for joy, the ritual can lead us, over time, to create a few more reasons to celebrate life.

The prayer seemed so appropriate to the moment. It was actually a part of what I would normally do at that point in the day. The mosque was one of the rooms in the house in which God dwelled. It didn't feel respectful to stand and recite prayers in Hebrew; I didn't think that my hosts were ready for that. Who was I kidding? Five minutes earlier, *I* hadn't been ready for that!

I knew that I could only be in the mosque with integrity if I used my own tradition. I couldn't pray in their words because they're not my words. I needed to push myself to enter their space, but could only do that if I had the comfort of entering into it on my terms, using the traditions that were familiar to me. I needed to use my particularity as a vehicle for universal connection, rather than choosing between the dignity of particularity and the dignity of universal connection.

I don't think anyone thought I had done a Cat Stevens—at least I hope they didn't. I was still Brad Hirschfield, an orthodox New York rabbi on his knees in that mosque. And this rabbi found that the simultaneous offering of Jewish and Islamic prayers formed a unity that was *bigger* than both of our traditions.

Syeed was bemused after the service was over. "We've had bishops here, and they're not so comfortable taking off their shoes," was his only comment. Apparently my esteemed Christian colleagues preferred to sit in the folding chairs in the foyer and observe. Entering each others' prayer rooms is new territory for all of us.

Syeed and I continued our conversation that afternoon in his office. Afternoon turned to evening and, lo and behold, guess what? The muezzin's voice rang out again, calling us to evening service.

This time I knelt next to Syeed and recited the Sh'ma, the centerpiece of Judaism's evening service. The words of the Sh'ma are from Deuteronomy, and proclaim the oneness of God—which was the same prayer Syeed and the rest of the men in the room recited: "There is no God but Allah."

It was pretty heavy. I spent ten minutes on my knees, reciting the Sh'ma over and over again, focusing on what it would be like if God were really one. What if we could really feel that bigness and rest in that wholeness. To be a true monotheist is to understand that no one human understanding of an infinite power can ever fully capture what that power is, or how, exactly, to relate to or honor it. To appreciate this is to become modest about claiming to know "what God wants."

The more traditionally religious you are, the more deeply modest and radically inclusive you should be. After all, if your tradition truly is the infinite gift of an infinite God, then how could there be only one way to understand it? In fact, the uniformity that we so often fight for as lovers, parents, nations, and religious traditions is the *opposite* of the infinite unity that inspires us most.

When I cherish the wisdom attained by others who have followed a different path, then I will find the unity that I seek. This does not mean I must agree with or approve of everything that everyone does, but it means that their successes, successes that I cannot attain because I am riding on a different train, are the context of my critique. So when I reflect on the pain that was caused by the Catholic Church over the last two thousand years, I also reflect on the healing that it brought by inviting people to sit week after week before the image of a crucified Christ, the image of someone who would suffer endlessly so that we might not have to, and promise that there is no pain from which one cannot recover. When I shudder at the absolutist strains of thought in Jewish and Muslim tradition that pursue the absolute truth that members of each claim to possess, I also sit awed by traditions that have, at different times, fearlessly embraced all manner of human inquiry because they believed that human beings really could know the absolute truth and were free to pursue it anywhere.

The only other time the Sh'ma is recited over and over, which is what I did during the evening service in Plainfield, is at the end of Yom Kippur, the Day of Atonement. Jews spend twenty-five hours (as if twenty-four were not enough) fasting, meditating, praying, and abstaining from bathing and making love. In effect, we play dead for that long day and reemerge reborn, certain that there is nothing that could not be forgiven from the perspective of an infinite, loving God.

That's why, for me at least, the holiest moment of Yom Kippur actually occurs after the day has ended, when we come back to life and break the fast. In my family, the vodka comes out of the freezer and the Scotch out of the liquor cabinet. We stand, raise our glasses, and shout, *"L'chayim!"* To life! We are back! We can start again and know that there is room for all of us.

Saying the Sh'ma on my knees next to Dr. Syeed in the mosque in Plainfield didn't stop the suicide bombers or the war in Iraq, but it affirmed that there really was something out there or deep within each of us that was truly big enough for all of us to share. When we work from that place—a place not of uniformity but of endless diversity—we will begin to find the kind of unity that will heal us and heal our world. We will figure out that the challenge is never how to get us all into a single room, but how to build structures with enough rooms for everyone, rooms in which to live out our lives safely and pursue the happiness to which we all aspire, with the awareness that standing in each of them comes with both challenges and gifts. It's not unlike my home in Riverdale, which has many rooms. I'm far more comfortable in my bedroom or the kitchen than in the basement or my thirteen-year-old daughter's room. But I know that without them all, it wouldn't be my home. And so it is with our world. We need everyone. All our faiths. All our differences.

I don't think Isaiah's mosquechurchagogue is a pipe dream—it is an expression of a deep longing that we all share. Too often we think that by making room for each other we are somehow surrendering our integrity, that integrity involves a pushing away, a discarding of beliefs and parts of ourselves that are false or compromised. But the word *integrity* has the same root as *integrate*. When we fight for the integrity of our beliefs, relationships, and communities, we are actually fighting to integrate that which seems alien or threatening. We will have the most integrity when we are integrating the widest range of people and ideas.

CHAPTER SEVEN

THE BISHOP OF

AUSCHWITZ

When the Whole Really Is Greater

Than the Sum of the Parts

I't's always a challenge to remember past hurts or traumas without becoming identified with them. When one of my daughters was four years old she was diagnosed with pediatric epilepsy. I had gone to pick her up from preschool, something that I rarely did. Calling to her once, twice, I knew something was wrong as she walked toward me. She didn't respond and had a remote, fixed gaze, in a world all of her own for about five seconds. Then she was back. She looked at me as if I had suddenly appeared. "Hi, Abba," she said with a big smile. I was scared, sad, and entirely confused. I had no idea what was going on, but I knew that what had just happened was abnormal. My usually fiery four-year-old had acted like a zombie. It was as if I were not there, as if nothing were there, and then she was back. It was as if a switch had been thrown that turned her "off" and then, seconds later, it had been thrown again and she was "on," back to her normal self.

"My daughter is an epileptic," I said to the doctor who had made the diagnosis. It was the first thing that popped into my mind.

"Your daughter is your daughter," she replied, a young woman roughly my age and a very dear friend. "She happens to have epilepsy."

I understood what she meant intellectually, but emotionally I wasn't really able to take it in until five years later. I had had an operation to remove a tumor from my lung, and someone referred to me as a "cancer survivor." *I'm not a cancer survivor*, I thought. *I'm just me.*

Terrible events should not be allowed to overtake your sense of who you are as an individual. You can become completely identified with the experience of "cancer survivor" or "Holocaust survivor." And you can start to see other people in that way, too.

We can't let ourselves be defined or define others based entirely on who we have been or what has happened in the past. Important as the past is, life is best when it's more about the present and the future.

This was one of the most important lessons that came out of the refounding of Hevre Lomdei Mishnayos, a synagogue in the Polish town of Oswiecim—better known outside of Poland for the past sixty years by its German name, Auschwitz—in the late 1990s. The synagogue, which had been a Hasidic prayer house before World War II, was located just a mile from the site of the infamous Nazi concentration camp.

The reclamation of the synagogue was carried out by a small group of people led by Fred Schwartz, affectionately known as "Fred the Furrier" from television commercials that had aired across the New York area in the 1970s and 1980s. I normally stay away from Holocaust projects. Why? I want to say this in as gentle and respectful a way as possible. I stay away because they too often perpetuate victim identity and suffering. Everyone wants to use the Holocaust for something. There's no business like Shoah business (not my line). That disturbs me. But the Furrier and his associates persuaded me to become involved. They didn't want a place that contained photos of bodies being bulldozed or permanent memorial candles. The synagogue would acknowledge the past without being enslaved by it. Their vision was of a building that would celebrate life in a place that was synonymous with death. *That* I couldn't resist.

The Furrier and his group formed a foundation to purchase, rehabilitate, reopen, and run the synagogue. It took years of organizational work and building relationships within the Polish and Israeli governments, American Holocaust groups, and the Catholic Church. It involved an unbelievable amount of choreography. They had to convince the Poles that resurrecting the synagogue would not embarrass them by highlighting the frightening proximity of the camp to the town, where life had continued normally throughout the war, at least compared with what had transpired nearby. They had to work with members of the Hasidic community, who had to accept the involvement of non-Hasidim in the restoration and use of a formerly Hasidic prayer hall. And, ultimately, they had to work with the State of Israel and survivor groups to garner support.

The focus of such groups is usually to remind the world of past horrors or extract repayment for them. There's a place for those tasks, but what Fred and friends were trying to do was substantially different. Holocaust groups generally see words like *recovery* and *reconciliation* as betraying their suffering or the suffering of their parents and grandparents. They are not ready to move to the next stage of loss, which is to reenter a life that is defined by more than the loss. That is why when you set foot in Holocaust waters, you set off a potential tidal wave of pain, anger, and fear. Everyone has an angle on what happened. Poles refuse to admit the ways in which they were complicit in the murder of Jews, in part because they feel that their own story of victimization will be undermined if they admit their complicity. Those of us who are most eager to hear Poles apologize need to make Poles feel protected. Isn't that usually the case? We often want to apologize, but need to know that if we admit our guilt we will not make ourselves too vulnerable, hurting ourselves by admitting that we hurt someone else.

Jews are afraid of relinquishing the uniqueness of their suffering. Jewish groups have protested at the National Holocaust Museum in Washington over exhibits dealing with the history of racism in America and the genocide in Rwanda. I guess we are not only trained to believe that others must be wrong for us to be right, but that the suffering of one community is more horrific if that which others have suffered is less so. It's as if suffering were a commodity and my admitting that you have some diminishes the value of mine. Talk about a bad use of supply and demand!

That thinking tends to dominate the world of Holocaust memory, but was resisted by Fred, Jim Schrieber, and Daniel Eisenstadt, an energetic and sophisticated young attorney, who were the core group in setting up the foundation to restore the synagogue. When I accompanied them to the synagogue's groundbreaking ceremony, we traveled to Poland via Berlin. Fred and Jim—through charm, political acumen, and perseverance—had arranged a dinner with Kurt Biedenkopf, the acting president of Germany; Michael Naumann, Germany's minister of culture; and members of the German Parliament. The dinner, held to commemorate the refounding of the synagogue, took place in the private restaurant that had been built on top of the newly reopened Reichstag, the German capitol building that had served as the seat of government under the Nazis.

When Jim and Fred had told me about the dinner weeks earlier in New York, in typical fashion yours truly had blurted out that the meal should include a Havdalah ceremony, the brief prayers that mark the end of the Jewish Sabbath and welcome in the new week. After all, wasn't that what the journey to Germany and back to Auschwitz was all about, I asked. Weren't we seeking to move to a new place in our relationship with the Holocaust and each other? Havdalah marks a new beginning, an opportunity to reenter the world and reengage in the work of making our world a better place. How could we not share the opportunity to declare that intention publicly?

Fred and Jim loved the idea and committed to making it happen. Little did I know what I had stumbled into. When I told people that I was heading to open a synagogue in Auschwitz and on the way I would be stopping in Berlin to lead Havdalah on top of the Reichstag, they looked at me as if I were crazy. And as Saturday evening approached, I began to think that they might be right.

When I emerged from the cab in front of the Reichstag's massive complex of buildings, I was sure they *were* right. An enormous German flag, illuminated by seemingly endless floodlights, billowed in the wind. What the hell was I thinking? Who did I think I was, to go marching into the building from which Adolf Hitler had led a movement that cost the lives of tens of millions of people—a movement dedicated to the eradication of the Jewish people wherever they were found—and lead a little Jewish ritual? I had been crazy to suggest it.

The feeling in the elegant candlelit room was celebratory, but in the few minutes that I had to get acclimated (having arrived late because I had waited to travel until Shabbat was over), it was clear that nobody was talking about what our group was doing there. It was like, "Okay, there's a group of Jews on their way to Poland to open a synagogue and they stopped by the Reichstag for a bite with the president." And that's when I got up in my dark suit, trying not to betray all of the confused emotions that I felt inside.

I admitted my own fears. I said that I felt it was important to do the ritual with the full awareness of who we were. All transitions are hard, I said. And our ability to make them is always in question. But, I continued, turn around and look out

the window. Look out over a united Berlin. If anyone had said
that the Berlin Wall would collapse, that the citizens of Germany
would one day be united in freedom, and that it could happen
without another world war, skeptics would have said that was
crazy, too. We have within us a greater capacity for overcoming
the pain of our pasts than we realize. We can make the walls
that divide us fall down, and we can come together to create
new realities that acknowledge history without being chained
by it. We are proving that tonight.

I asked the president and Isaac, a member of our group
who had survived Auschwitz, to come forward. I placed the
multi-wicked Havdalah candle into the president's hands, explaining that it represented the sacred potential of the world of
work. After twenty-five hours of rest from doing and making,
we light a candle whose fire represents, as it does in so many
cultures, our ability to create and build. Think of the gods' anger
at Prometheus for stealing fire from them and thus empowering
the human race. With the lighting of the Havdalah candle, we
proclaim that far from stealing from the gods, it is our sacred
obligation to create and build our world.

I asked the president to remember that Germany holds
many dark memories for people throughout the world, but that
Germans could continue the transformation of that darkness
into light, as they had when they brought down the Wall.

Turning to Isaac, I asked him to hold the sweet spices that
are, with the kindling of flame, a symbol of welcoming a new
week into the world. I thanked him for standing with us and
proclaiming from this spot that life could be as sweet as the
spices he now held, if we breathed in deeply and searched out

the opportunities for such sweetness even in the most unex-
pected places, places like the building in which he now stood.
With that, I raised a cup of wine and pronounced the blessing
that thanks the Creator for the fruit of the vine. I reminded all
of us that wine does not grow on vines; it requires human partnership to unleash the full potential of all that we find in the
world around us. Then, pronouncing the final blessing that wel-
comes in the new week, I asked that everyone in the room thank
each other for their partnership in creating a new week that
would become part of a new world.

Isaac stroked the back of my head in a grandfatherly way
as I did this, and I began to cry. The chance to move past re-
membering nightmares and begin creating dreams was why I
had come on this trip, and it was beginning to be a reality. Of
course, the road to that reality is filled with bumps, as I was soon
to find out.

Naumann took me downstairs to the Bundestag, where
the German Parliament meets (and met during the years of
Nazi rule). Over the chamber hangs an enormous eagle. "That
is what we call the strangled chicken," said Naumann, "because
it is such a ridiculous thing."

At that moment, after all my pontificating at the dinner
above, I realized how far we still had to go. The eagle, almost
as much as the swastika, was the symbol under which the Nazis
fought. If I had had more courage, I would have said to Naumann, "Say anything but that." Self-effacing jokes are not the
way to handle your reappropriation of what to many people is a
very powerful and painful symbol. Tell me you keep the eagle
here in the place where you make your laws not because you

long to return to an era of racism and hatred, but because you appreciate that no people should have to completely excise its past in order to move into the future. You would be right, and it might even be the best way to rinse the hate from the symbol and fill it with the meaning that would flow from its use in a new, free, and united Germany. In fact, that might have been the very reason I wanted to celebrate Havdalah on the roof of the Reichstag—because now, for at least some of us, this building would always be connected to a memory of which we could all be proud, not only to memories of pain. I would have said, "Michael, tell me the whole complicated truth instead of sharing a simple joke, and we'll all be better off."

That's what I should have said, but I didn't. And even if I had, I'm not sure that enough of us are ready to accept that kind of honesty from those who have hurt us to make good on my promise that he would be properly heard when he used that approach. In the end, that approach depends as much on the openness of the one receiving a complex truth as on the courage of the one we ask to share it.

Our group traveled the next day to Warsaw and from there to Krakow. That evening, Asher, one of the Israelis who had joined us, mentioned to me that there would be a morning prayer service the following day in a suite belonging to one of the Hasidim who had traveled from New York to be at the groundbreaking ceremonies. At 6:30 a.m. the following day, I walked into the suite, where a dozen men had gathered to pray. I could feel the tension in the room rise. There were ten Hasidim with beards and long coats, and there was Asher—himself a Yiddish-speaking survivor of Auschwitz (something that connected him to the others in the room)—and there was I, a fourth-generation American rabbi with long hair tied back in a ponytail, and no long coat!

I don't even think that they were angry about my presence, as much as completely shocked that I would choose to join them and that I actually knew what I was doing. Later on, one of the Hasidim, himself the son-in-law of a man who had grown up in the building adjoining the Auschwitz synagogue, asked me how it was that I was so comfortable with the service and its rituals. When I explained to him that I actually prayed the same words that he did every morning, he was genuinely shocked. Like most of us, myself included, he made assumptions about my inner life based on my appearance.

Familiarity in appearance is comforting, of course, and it grounds us. It lets us quickly assess the people around us, and signals to us what we can expect of them, whether we're a room full of men wearing the same long coats and beards or a room full of lawyers all wearing their Brooks Brothers suits and same-color "power tie" of the moment. But it can be hurtful to rely too heavily on the need for familiarity. Just ask anyone who's ever been pulled over for DWB—driving while black.

The deep sense of sadness I felt when the room full of Hasidim stiffened was not from the feeling of being excluded, pushed away, or disapproved of (although I felt all those things). We were on our way to a place where human beings were gassed and burned because they were Jewish or gay or because of their political beliefs. We had figured out how we could all die together—or at least it was figured out for us. But there was a genuine question whether we could pray together—or, even more important, *live* together. It felt as though even within our one little community we were not prepared to make the turn into the new week and the new world that I had celebrated in Berlin. That made me sad. Maybe I was naïve, perhaps I was expecting too much too fast. Their coldness hurt me because I respect and appreciate their deep knowledge and their rigorous, inspired Judaism.

We let down our guard among those with whom we feel most comfortable. I am amazed by my children's ability to behave perfectly with other people, but to make me nuts when it's just our family. Becky, who has been a teacher and now is a school administrator, tells me not to worry—that's normal. She worries when a kid is perfect at home but acts out in school. Kids *should* feel safe to blow off steam at home, with those upon whom they can rely most. At least that's what I told myself in the room of Hasidim to cheer myself up.

In the end, the moment of distrust passed, and we prayed.

Of course, these kinds of internecine tensions are not limited to any one faith or community. Christians, Muslims, Hindus, and Buddhists all behave in the same way. We have all mobilized our sense of the sacred to sever someone else's sense of the sacred when it is different from our own. Sunnis consider Shia apostate and vice versa, which leads them to justify murdering each other. People are told that they are no longer Catholic because they support the ordination of women priests or the use of birth control within the context of a Catholic family. I won't even go near what happens in communities struggling with how to approach honoring the full dignity of their gay members—if they even consider the idea of doing so.

This type of behavior is not limited to religion. The brutal language that dominates contemporary politics drives most eligible voters away from the polls, especially young voters, despite the fact that Americans between eighteen and thirty-five years of age report intense interest in the big issues that confront our nation. It's not that they don't care, as is so often claimed, but that they care so much that it seems politics has become too mean-spirited and small-minded to address issues of real importance. I often wonder if the same isn't true for most Americans, more than ninety percent of whom believe in some higher power, but so many of whom have a hard time connecting to that power through traditional religious affiliation.

The synagogue's groundbreaking took place in September of 2000. The event had made international news, and the crowd was so large that enormous tents had been erected over Karpka Square. Dignitaries representing the governments of Poland, Israel, and the United States had gathered. Prince Hassan of Jordan was there. The prince is a tireless advocate for the dignity of all faiths and the need to build better bridges between them.

It was a beautiful, sunny day, the kind that you don't associate with Auschwitz—but even there the sun did not stop shining. There were giant yellow awnings (a strange color choice for the fabric that was sheltering us, since yellow stars had been the Nazi identification mark for so many millions of Jews) erected over the square. People were dressed in their best clothing. There was excitement in the air. Within the synagogue, wafting out over the proceedings, there was the aroma of a full kosher lunch waiting for us. The food had been flown in from an Eastern European–style kosher deli in Teaneck, New Jersey! Talk about the struggle over what makes something authentic. Restaurants in Warsaw and Krakow specialize in the food that Jews ate before the war, although none of it is kosher. Of course, not all those Jews kept kosher, either. Once again the lesson of multiple authenticities showed itself. The lunch was totally authentic according to a three-thousand-year-old system of Jewish dietary laws. And it also would have been authentic if instead of ordering fried chicken from Teaneck, New Jersey, we had ordered kishka from a restaurant in Warsaw. (Kishka, a typical Polish-Jewish dish, is made with matzo meal, grated potatoes, garlic, and onions fried in schmaltz—chicken fat—and stuffed into a casing of intestines. It's a free ticket for a trip to the cardiologist!)

There were speeches, blessings, and stories describing life in Oswiecim before the war. Catholic Poles performed who had devoted their careers to learning the Yiddish and Hebrew music that was sung by Polish Jews before the war. The organizers of the event movingly, and perhaps a little eerily, showed that a new day was dawning.

At the conclusion of the ceremony, the bishop of the area around Oswiecim, a man named Ricoczy, announced that he would celebrate a special mass in the town's main church, which was across the street from the synagogue. He was a rather ordinary-looking older man who had said little during the groundbreaking ceremony and didn't look at all comfortable about being on the dais with the other dignitaries, or with meeting me, or with much of anything else that went on around him.

Talk about groundbreaking. This was not to be missed. Oceans of ink have been spilled analyzing the church's supersessionist theology (the making of a second covenant of Christianity that supersedes the old covenant God made with the Jews), which proclaimed Judaism passé, and established the church's claim that the Jewish people were eternally guilty for killing Jesus. Both of those claims contributed to the rise of Nazism and the ease with which its genocidal mission was tolerated by European Christians. I felt privileged to live at a moment when that same church proclaimed, even at the local level, that we were past that and a synagogue being reopened in Poland was a spiritually significant event that demanded attention and support. But like everything else that had happened on this trip, it was not simple.

Precisely at the same time when we had been invited to cross the square in one direction to enter the church, a contingent of our group was crossing the square in the other direction to say the afternoon prayer on the site of what would be our reclaimed synagogue. It was assumed, of course, that anyone who would want to attend the mass would want nothing to do with the afternoon service, and vice versa.

I didn't want to insult anybody, but I wanted to do both! Jews and Christians might be going in opposite directions physically (one group to the synagogue, the other to the church) but they were actually traveling in the same direction spiritually. Each was turning to the tradition with which it was most comfortable in order to access the deeper meaning of what had transpired that day. Each was going to a place of comfort that would help them sort out their feelings, provide perspective, and build hope. That's why, for me, doing both made sense. It was two sides of the same coin, and I thought, *Why not enjoy the beauty of each side?* I realize that not everyone wants both sides, and that's fine, too. But imagine how it would change the experience of worship, whether it happens in a church, a synagogue, or a mosque, while hiking the Grand Canyon, or watching the kids in your backyard, or in the halls of a museum—all places of inspiration. Each experience of being inspired by something particular would deepen not only our connection to that particular place or practice, but to all people seeking inspiration throughout the world, wherever and however they were seeking it. It would not make the differences go away, but would create a common bond among all those who are different. That's what I was wanting and seeking.

Fred and Aileen Schwartz and Wendy and Jim Schrieber also decided that they wanted to go to mass, but they, too, appreciated the importance of participating in the afternoon service at the synagogue. So, while people were going over to the church and getting ready for that service to begin, we journeyed across Karpka Square with a small group that was headed for the synagogue. I also thought this was a good thing because it would allow us to walk into the church a bit late, with relative anonymity, and occupy unobtrusive seats in back. We weren't looking to make a statement, or draw attention to the fact that none of the Polish Jewish leaders were planning to attend. To be sure, there were no Catholics heading to Hevre Lomdei Mishnayos, either! In fact, most people just hung out in the square, which does raise the issue of which place—the synagogue, the church, or the square itself—was the real sacred space that afternoon. They all were, of course, each in its own way.

The afternoon service had a special kind of power for me. As we began to pray, I was struck by the normalcy of it all. Here we were, a mile from the most infamous of the Nazi concentration camps, saying the same words from Psalms that I say every afternoon: "How good it is to dwell in your house, O Lord." On the one hand, the ritual of it was comforting, like always wearing the same shirt to a football game, or eating turkey at Thanksgiving. Not to mention the power of speaking about the beauty of God's House as we made one such house beautiful. But on the other hand, I also thought that any God worth praying to, who really is responsible for our world, was also responsible for what had happened just down the road. If the God I was praying to was not responsible for Auschwitz, then what was I doing praying?

I've been all over the spectrum on what kind of God it is that I think that I'm praying to, but I've found that in my life prayer has value in and of itself to the person who prays. It's not as much about changing God's mind as it is about changing our own mind, which in the end is the only thing we can control anyway. It doesn't really matter who or what you pray to, but keeping up that conversation with whatever it is that's larger than ourselves, really works. It links the experiences of our personal lives to the larger rhythms of time and tradition as it did that afternoon. It pushes us to open our hearts and share what's most deeply there. And it provides moments into which we can retreat from the noise of everything else in our lives.

The afternoon service was about the spirituality of the normal, of anchoring oneself in the everyday, in the routine and the ritual and the present moment in a situation fraught with insidious little conflicts and dark voices coming out of the ground, disturbing echoes from the past.

I was torn as our group of five walked over to the church. I knew that in going I would be stepping on a lot of toes. Most orthodox Jews will not even set foot inside a church. And while it's one thing to break that prohibition for a friend's child's christening or wedding, in this case I was going in a way that could be particularly offensive: Poles, virtually all of whom are Catholics, helped camps like Auschwitz to exist, and there is no shortage of stories from survivors about their particularly fierce anti-Semitism. As I write this, I am also compelled to note that a million Poles died in Auschwitz, and that the Jewish experience of victimization has blinded too many Jews to the fact that Poles were also victims. Not to mention those Poles who risked their lives and the lives of their families to save Jews from the Nazis. Would I risk my kids in order to save someone else's? It's easy to say yes, but who can know until we stand in that place?

But, of course, it wasn't just that which drew me across the street and into the church. The mass was being celebrated in memory of the victims of the Holocaust. The bishop was affirming that the day we reopened a synagogue in the city of Oswiecim, it was important to Catholics as well as Jews. I felt that that deserved to be honored. The bishop had recognized that the whole community was served by a renewed Jewish presence there. He understood that the reopening of Hevre Lomdei Mishnayos was not only a triumph for Jews, but a triumph for decency, reconciliation, and renewal. Human values that deserved to be celebrated in a Catholic way because they were as much Catholic as they were Jewish, as they were *human*. The adjectives describe how the values get celebrated, not to whom they belong. Whether by insight or intuition, Bishop Ricoczy was emerging as the perfect model of faith without fanaticism.

The fanatic can only enjoy the game when his team wins, whether his team is The Catholic Church or the Red Sox, his synagogue or the Chicago Bears. The fanatic makes no distinction between what he loves, what he does, and what is right, but the one who locates deep faith without the fanaticism remains devoted to his "team" while embracing the sport as a whole. He knows that what he loves is a part of something larger, which he loves as well. A die-hard Knicks fan could still applaud Michael Jordan's amazing performances at the Garden and cheer his beautiful play. That was how I felt about Bishop Ricoczy's offering of a mass to commemorate the synagogue's groundbreaking.

The five of us walked across the square that had been renamed, after the fall of the Iron Curtain, for Father Karpka, a Catholic priest who had championed good relations with Oswiecim's Jewish community before the war and was himself a victim of the Nazis. The town itself was gray and depressed. It would have been working-class if anyone had been working, and it was painfully poor.

Oswiecim's kids, as I learned between the groundbreaking and the reopening of the synagogue, wanted to establish a disco in a former factory that had been turned, during the war, into a slave labor site. There was the predictable uproar. This group

and that group thought the idea was sacrilegious. An outrage!
How could people, kids no less, think of dancing till dawn and
partying in a building where people had been worked to death
by the Nazis?

But my feeling was—how wonderful! And I championed
the idea. Talk about reclaiming life from the jaws of death! If
anything can be called sacred revenge, it was this disco, a place
of dancing and music in a town where the only thing to do after
dark was get drunk and break things.

To persuade my Jewish brethren, I deployed the Talmud
(heavy artillery), which says that the Romans destroyed the Second Temple in Jerusalem in 70 C.E. because of *sinat hinam*, which
translates as "free hatred" or "purposeless hatred." The rabbis
situate their discussion of this institutional collapse in a volume
whose primary focus is divorce law. They knew that what was
true for the institution called the temple was true for the institution of marriage. The ancient rabbis understood that no institution can be stronger than the relationships between the people
who are a part of it.

Rabbi Kook, commenting on the text almost two thousand years later, talks about the necessary response to *sinat
hinam* as "free love," or "purposeless love." In the same way that
we have it within us to make hate our default response, he
taught that every person has the capacity to make love the default response. Just as hate can flow intuitively, without waiting
for a rationale, so can love. It's actually the same response mech-
anism, and it's up to us which emotion it carries. Rabbi Kook
suggests that unconditional love might be the only reasonable

response to unconditional hate, since both are irrational. It's not that we *need* to dispense with reason, but if we do, wouldn't it be great if we irrationally loved instead of irrationally hating?

Maybe the best response to the unconditional silence of the slave labor factory in Oswiecim was unconditional dancing and music. The disco could be a very holy place—a place that was filled with life after being totally identified with death. A place that had been pseudonymous with repression and forced labor could be transformed into a place of free expression and unrestrained celebration.

This is not to say that I didn't understand or respect the people who opposed the use of the factory for the disco. Any survivor of the Holocaust, or of any genocidal war, for that matter, has been in hell and has the right to make anything he or she wants thereafter on earth. We owe them all latitude in our response to their judgments. But we do not have to limit ourselves to forever thinking like those who have survived in order to honor either them or the victims who did not. We have choices about how life should proceed in the face of tragedy. In acknowledging our power to make such choices, we affirm our reentry into life. When we fail to imagine that we have choices—that how it has always been is how it must always be—we continue to be victims of those who sought our destruction.

The church was a big building, musty and a bit dilapidated. The parishioners, of which there were at least a couple of hundred, hadn't seen a new suit or topcoat in a long, long time. It was a room full of people who knew that the service was being convened for the new synagogue. Our presence in the town had created a response that was modestly positive, although the general friendliness and curiosity had been punctuated by occasional hostility. Every once in a while someone would spit on you. I really don't know why they spat. They were not exactly eager to talk. Perhaps they were suspicious about what we really wanted. Perhaps, as some suggested, they really did hate it that the Jews were back in town. Perhaps they were simply angry at us for dredging up old and painful memories, and didn't know how to say that.

Two young guys, seminarians or altar boys in ritual garments, came running to the back of the church when they saw us enter, and gestured for us to follow them. We walked toward the altar. So much for being less than obvious, I thought. There were icons and gold plate everywhere. A crucifix was hung above the altar on which a golden chalice sat.

I thought the young men would seat us in the front pews, but no! They led Fred, Jim, and me to seats that had been reserved at the altar itself, with the clergy. Fred's and Jim's wives were seated up front, facing us.

The service began with lots of organ music and Polish hymns. Although it was hardly my first church service, it was the first time that I was experiencing Holocaust memory through another spiritual community. In some ways it was the exact opposite of the service I had just left across the street, where everything was familiar. In the church, everything felt new and strange. There I had been a member of the family, but in the church I felt like an outsider.

Bishop Ricoczy rose to give the homily. Most of his talk was in Polish, but at one point it was translated into English. "We are gathered here not for the dignity of those who were murdered," the bishop said. "Their place in heaven is guaranteed because of what they endured. We are here to ensure our own dignity. If we don't remember *all of them*," he said this very slowly and with great emphasis, "then it is our place in heaven and our dignity that are in peril."

I was blown away. To believe as a Catholic that one's place in heaven depends in any way on memorializing Jewish victims of the Holocaust is amazing. Ricoczy was teaching all of us that the success of our respective communities could not be measured only by the success of its members—that the real test lay in our sense of connection with and obligation to those beyond our church or tribe. He was offering a living theology that embodied the blessing that God gave to Abraham: through you shall all people of the world be blessed. When other people feel blessed that your people are in this world, then you will be blessed, or, in the bishop's words, find heaven—whether you think that's here on earth or someplace else.

We came to the point in the service where the members of the congregation formally greet one another and offer good wishes and acknowledge and celebrate the moment. The blessing is often "Peace be upon you" (which I knew from having been at mass a few times in the past). Almost as a joke, Jim, Fred, and I said *Shalom aleichem*—the Hebrew of precisely those words, and a common Jewish greeting in any setting. The young priest seated next to me turned to me grudgingly and said, "A blessing on you." There was an aura of coldness and reserve about him, and I clearly felt that he wasn't one hundred percent certain that he liked what was happening.

I was feeling all this when I was shocked to notice the

bishop making a beeline toward me. I was totally unprepared for what happened next. He took my hands in his hands and looked deep into my eyes and said, not in Polish, not in English, but in Hebrew, *Shalom.*

I was blown away. What a teacher this man was. This greeting process was part of his liturgy, recited in Poland for a thousand years. In its midst, he was using Hebrew. It was unbelievable. He was telling me, *I'll extend myself to you; I know you can't fully participate here, but I will help you feel more yourself in my space.*

I was overwhelmed. I felt tears running down my face. I had been moved by the translated portion of his homily, which was a heroic and beautiful theology. But this gesture went from being theological to personal. I grasped his forearms, holding him tightly, unable to speak.

I don't remember the next five or ten minutes, but at the end of the service, as people left the church, there was another shock. The bells in the tower were playing the Hebrew song *Heiveinu Shalom Aleichem*, which means "We bring peace to you."

Can you imagine: a Polish-Catholic church in spitting distance of the most infamous of the camps, playing a Hebrew melody on its bells? And a bishop who had gone out of his way to find a Hebrew song that best reflected the Jewish perspective on the need for healing from the people or entity that actually bore some very real responsibility for the anti-Semitism without which Auschwitz could never have been conceived, let alone built?

The bishop wasn't worried about preserving what was Catholic in the face of our Jewish incursion. He knew that honoring the Jews, both living and dead, in his church and at this charged site wouldn't make him or his tradition less real or challenge its integrity. In his understanding, we didn't have to be wrong for him to be right.

I didn't want to leave that church. I wanted to stay, and not just because they were playing our song. How had he thought to do this, I marveled. Where did he have to go to get the sheet music for the bell master? These were profoundly spiritual acts.

The ringing bells were neither a betrayal of his tradition nor a usurping of mine. He was finding himself more deeply through my experience, embodying a truth that is as old as our beginning—that we find our best self in relationship.

The oldest question in the Bible is, "Where are you?" which God asks Adam and Eve after they have eaten from the tree of good and evil. Neither Adam nor Eve answers that question. It would be twenty generations until it was answered by Abraham, the master journeyer. But that day, Bishop Ricoczy answered that eternal question and proclaimed, like Abraham, "Here I am," and was telling me that his person and presence were richer because his declaration had to do with finding where I was.

It could be argued that the whole Bible is an answer to that one question: "Where are you?" We so often find ourselves—are able to locate truly who we are—by finding each other. Finding yourself is not some self-obsessed, narcissistic, postmodern pursuit. It's the purpose of life's journey. And so is the recognition that we find our best self in relationship to others.

Which is one of the things that the Bible is telling us when it says to "love your neighbor as yourself." This teaching is always talked about as if it were directing us to love our neighbor. But it's not about being nice and sweet to everyone. It's telling us that you have to love yourself first, really love who you are, *to be able* to love someone else. If you think you've learned to love yourself but can't love other people, you're mistaken. The test of loving yourself is that you are able to love others more fully.

That was what the bishop was doing. He embodied the teaching that you don't become less when you reach out and incorporate pieces of me. We think that we must choose between independence (the model of strength and health) or dependence (the model of weakness and underdevelopment). But the notion of loving our neighbors as ourselves, the model of Bishop Ricoczy, is the model of interdependence. We recognize the absolute necessity of our individual needs, desires, styles, and traditions while embracing the awareness that the depth of all of them will be reached through our relationships with others. The test of our integrity is actually its permeability. When our hearts and minds are genuinely open to one another, when we are truly seeking, we uncover the best in all of us. If that was possible in Auschwitz, it is surely possible anywhere.

CHAPTER EIGHT

ADAM AND EVE WERE

NOT THE COSBYS

Learning That You Don't Have to

Disconnect Because You Disagree

WHEN I RETURNED TO THE UNITED STATES TO ENTER THE University of Chicago after I became disillusioned with the settlement movement in Israel, one of the things that struck me was the enormous popularity of *The Cosby Show*. The Cosbys were the Ozzie and Harriet of the 1980s. They were a rich, perfect black family. Bill Cosby played Heathcliff "Cliff" Huxtable, an ever-patient doctor dad with a small family practice based in his beautiful Brooklyn brownstone so he could be available as a father to his kids. Cliff's wife, Clair, was a wildly successful, high-powered attorney who had broken through the glass ceiling and gotten off the mommy track but still managed to be a perfect mom. This is the life we all dream of, but don't have unless we're on massive doses of Xanax or Prozac. The Cosbys were in every way, according to Wikipedia, the "utterly typical traditional American sitcom family."

The show was a fantasy, but it was a really important fantasy. It corrected decades of images of blacks on television whose roles had always revolved around singing and dancing, playing sports, or going to prison. So we ended up with fantasy.

Fantasies are not necessarily a bad thing. You don't need to be Sigmund Freud to appreciate the value of a good fantasy. Fantasies can heighten our expectations and stimulate our aspirations. The idea that we can focus our attentions not only on how things are, but on how they could be, even if we have no idea how to get there, is one of our most magnificent qualities as human beings. Fantasy differentiates us from both animals and angels. While it was once thought that toolmaking was the *sine qua non* of being human, primatologists have shown that chimpanzees use sticks as tools to get termites out of their mounds. Language was thought to be the true marker of our humanness until marine biologists uncovered the secret language of dolphins. But fantasy? That is ours alone. Even the angels, according to Jewish mystical tradition, are incapable of fantasy. They are created to perform a specific task; they don't wonder about alternatives, flights of fancy, and possibilities.

To fantasize is to appreciate that we are not bound by the circumstances in which we find ourselves. But it's also important to appreciate that we're not failures when our fantasies aren't realized. Some people, I'm sure, watched *The Cosby Show* and felt like failures as husbands, wives, or parents. Others immersed themselves in *The Cosby Show* as a palliative against the pain of their real lives. This, of course, is what happens when fantasy becomes a problem, when it becomes a substitute for life as we know it instead of a stimulant to our spirit.

The *Cosby Show* was not my show when I was growing up—*All in the Family* was. On Saturday nights, as my mom and dad would prepare to go out for the evening, we watched a racist, a dingbat, their imbecilic daughter, and their overly passionate meathead son-in-law fight about the most important issues of the day in an overcrowded house at 704 Houser Street in Queens, New York.

My younger brother and I would sit in my parents' large bedroom that was dominated by a king-size bed, which served not only as their sleeping space but as our trampoline. Far from being their inner sanctum, until they went to bed it was a place where we gathered to watch television, play board games, and hang out. It was, like most of our house, a warm place to be.

There was nothing threatening to me when Archie, Edith, Gloria, and the Meathead went at it. My parents loved each other. My mother was a divorcée who had endured an unhappy marriage for ten years. When she met my father, she was ready to love and be loved for who she was—the way I hope my daughters will one day be loved by their mates (only my wife can answer how I do in that department, but at least I try). My father married relatively late in life for that era and his social circle. He was old enough to know what he wanted, and looked forward to creating a life with the only person with whom I think he was ever really in love.

As the marriage developed, I'm sure they kept the lesson

close that my father passed on to me when I called him that night early on in my own marriage after Becky and I fought: you love people not only because of certain things, but despite certain things. They both really understood that, my father more than my mother, who, like me, is a romantic. In fact, I don't think that any relationship can be sustained for what is now approaching fifty years unless you do appreciate that you love each other not only because of who you are, but despite certain things as well. I don't think unconditional love exists between people. But if we accept that we will not always feel loving to the people we love, then anything is possible. The paradoxical nature of love is such that if our expectations of those we love are too idealized, it's unlikely that we'll be able to sustain even realistic long-term relationships. If our expectations are more realistic, on the other hand, then we have a shot at reaching our ideals.

My parents didn't hide their disagreements. Our house was filled with voices. Sometimes they were sweet and close; sometimes they were loud and angry. Real people have real disagreements, my parents told us. We don't love each other less because of them. They showed us that you don't have to disconnect because you disagree.

That lesson is not always easy to put into practice day by day in our lives. I have learned this the hard way in my marriage—especially around the struggles my wife and I have had around the illness of Dini, our youngest daughter.

When Dini, who is now five, was just ten weeks old, we were in Aspen for my annual teaching stint/family vacation. The first night there, Dini was screaming and feverish. Becky took her to the hospital while I stayed home with the other two girls. The emergency room doctor at Aspen Valley Medical Center was concerned about an infection, but nothing turned up in the initial tests, so she underwent a lumbar puncture, a spinal tap. Again, nothing. She was given a dose of antibiotics and seemed better.

"Has your daughter always had this much of a heart murmur?" asked the doctor the day after the spinal at a routine exam to which my wife went alone.

"I aged ten years in that moment," Becky told me.

We had to determine whether Dini's heart had become infected, a condition called endocarditis, which is not a good thing, particularly in an infant. The doctor recommended an echocardiogram—and quickly. The echocardiogram needed to be read by a pediatric cardiologist. There were none in Aspen or the nearby mountain towns. We considered taking Dini to Children's Hospital in Denver, or flying her back to New York.

Becky and I were pretty worried, as you can imagine. I called Michael, a physician friend in Denver who had studied with me in the past.

"Give me two hours," he said. "As it happens, there is an infectious disease conference going on in Aspen now. Let me make a few calls."

Another friend said, "We'll get you a private plane and fly her to Denver, if that's what you want to do."

Michael called back. "The head of pediatric infectious diseases at Denver Children's Hospital is in Aspen at the conference," he said. "He wants you to call him. Let me give you his cell phone number."

I punched in the number with trembling fingers. "Michael said I might be able to speak to you . . ."

"Are you the rabbi with the sick kid?"

"Yes," I said, my voice shaking. "We were told she might have an infection, then a heart murmur, then maybe endocarditis . . ."

"Where are you staying?"

"The Gant."

"What building?"

I told him our condo number.

"Walk out your front door," he said. He was standing across the hall from me. "I'm Harley. Why don't you hang up the cell phone, and we'll sit down and talk.

"This is not, obviously, something that you hope for, but it doesn't have to be devastating," Harley said. "The question is, do we need to get you to Denver to do the echocardiogram or can it be done up here? Let me make a few calls."

I went back to our condo and Harley soon called. "You don't have to go to Denver," he said. "I've asked that one of our pediatric cardiologists at Children's Hospital meet you in Glenwood Springs. I'm entirely comfortable with him performing the exam and giving you information about your daughter." Two hours before, Harley had been a stranger, and now he was interrupting his extraordinarily busy life to take care of my family.

Dini had started the antibiotics, so we were able to wait two days to go to Glenwood Springs for the echocardiogram.

The doctor came in, a cold, businesslike man in his mid-forties, dressed in scrubs.

"Undress the baby and lay her down on the examining table," he commanded.

"Can I hold her?" asked Becky.

"No."

The instant Dini left Becky's arms, she started to cry and then wail as the nurse pinned her on the table and smeared gel across her chest. Dr. Doom, as I had come to think of him, ran a wandlike apparatus over her tiny heart, studying the images that materialized on a screen. He stiffened and a look came over his face that I never want to see again. That's when *I* aged ten years.

Dini was shrieking and Becky was weeping and the doctor was as cold as ice. On his face was an expression as though he had seen the angel of death enter the room and hover over my ten-week-old baby girl. I couldn't breathe. Finally I saw his shoulders relax and he turned to me and said, "This is going to be okay. Let's get her dressed and we'll talk."

When Dini was dressed and quiet and back in Becky's arms, and we had composed ourselves (at least somewhat), the doctor said, "What I see is a fairly significant atrial septal defect, a hole between two chambers in her heart. But that is all we're looking at."

"I saw your expression," I said. "What else did you see?"

"Nothing else. Your daughter does not need a heart transplant. She may need to have this repaired when you get back to New York. But before anyone cracks her chest, I want you to talk to me. I'm prepared to say that all she needs is a stent. We can close this gap mechanically. So this is actually a very good day for you."

That's when I lost it. I was completely overwhelmed.

"No one wants to take her heart out of her chest," my wife said, crying with relief when we were back in the car. Dini was conked out in back, exhausted by the exam. I was crying, too—but for different reasons.

"Are you fucking nuts!" I said through my tears. "Our baby has a bad heart! And you're filled with joy!"

She was being a Pollyanna. And I was being ridiculous. But in the five and a half years since that morning in Glenwood Springs, we have never deviated from those basic postures. And each of those postures has helped us get through whatever it is that we've needed to deal with when it comes to our kids. My inclination has been to see the challenges and feel the pain longer and more deeply than Becky. Her impulse has been to focus on all of the good news we have received from the list of doctors that seemed to keep growing over the first years of our daughter's life. She sees the potential of Dini's life and feels the blessing that she is with us and alive. There is wisdom in both of those positions. I generally find Becky too upbeat, and she generally finds me too negative. But through our travails I have been in desperate need of her optimism and she has needed my willingness to confront the dark side.

We can't resolve our difficulties by making our differences go away. For big difficulties we have had to struggle to figure out how our differences complement each other. When Becky's relentless optimism is not driving me crazy, I find through her the strength and courage to forge ahead. The trait that hassles me most turns out also to be the one that heals me most. The trait that most aggravates me is also the one I most need. If she were more like me, I'd be dead—forget Dini.

The Bible teaches us that this is the way it has always been between men and women, and between human brings generally. In the relationship of the first couple, we see that the nature of human connection is complex and fraught.

Ezer k'negdo, Genesis says of Adam's future companion, Eve. These words are persistently mistranslated from the Hebrew into English in all the different versions of the Bible. In the King James Bible, for example, Eve is created as a "helpmeet" for Adam. In the Jewish Publication Society edition, considered one of the closest translations from the Hebrew into English, *ezer k'negdo* is translated as "a help to match him." But this still does not quite capture what the Hebrew says. The literal translation of *ezer k'negdo* is "a helper who is *against him.*"

Is this a mistake? I don't think so.

Every human relationship has its moments of hurt. Even in the most loving of marriages, it is always the case that the partners will hurt each other. To marry is hard—as each of us who has married has discovered. President George W. Bush was fond of saying, "People are either with us or against us." But I think Genesis is telling us that perhaps it is possible to be both at once.

The fact is, it may be that our most painful disagreements arise because we share the same values. The other day two young women, students at Smith College and very, very close friends, came into my office. Sarah is Palestinian; Becka is Jewish. They look nothing alike, yet they both wore jeans and carried back-packs with trailing iPod cords. Each possesses the gentle confidence that comes from being bright, secure, and well educated.

Becka's father, a friend and board member of CLAL, had become concerned with the tension in the relationship between the two girls. Sarah had been to visit relatives in the occupied territories and, on her return, had written a pretty savage blog, full of outrage, condemning Israel for conditions there. Becka, intuitively supportive of Israel, had been furious. Neither one of them had any interest in apologizing or relinquishing her views.

Prior to this incident they had had the kind of relationship where they could say anything to each other, nothing was out of bounds, and they were the closest of confidants. But this they found so volatile that they couldn't talk about it without the conversation quickly escalating into the kind of tension and hurt that tore them up inside and that they regretted but seemed powerless to control.

Their solution was to push the disagreement into the background, "to put it," as Becka said, "aside." Things had gotten better between them, but they both recognized and felt disappointed that there was a dark, painful place that lurked just under the surface of their friendship, which they had to skirt.

I had read Sarah's blog. "I could explain the ways in which you are one hundred percent right about everything you wrote," I told her. "Would that be a good thing to do in this case?"

"It wouldn't be bad," said Sarah.

"But that would make you right and Becka wrong. Are you so certain that is how it is? Because I could also explain the hundred ways in which your focus is too narrow and how, for all the right reasons, you have reached all of the wrong conclusions about what is really going on in that part of the world."

"But I only wrote what I saw," Sarah objected.

"But it may be that what you saw was not all that there was to see. It may be that you are confusing honesty and integrity with accuracy and completeness. It may be that your disagreement is less about particular sets of facts, which each of you could marshal to prove your respective points of view without making either of you feel better, than it is about a set of values which you both share."

I tried to get them to see that it was *because* they shared the same values that they were at loggerheads. If Becka hadn't felt in some way her friend's sense of outrage and injustice, there would have been nothing to fight about. She would simply have said, "Israel is right, and who cares what you think." And if Sarah hadn't known that no matter what her politics, or the context of life in the territories, suicide bombing and other acts of terror are wrong, she could have ignored Becka's indignation and outrage.

"Things have gotten a little better between you by putting this painful disagreement aside," I said. "But maybe what you really need to do is take it in and acknowledge it fully. Which would include how much you care for each other and how much you mean to each other and how many values you share."

Too often, peace between nations or people is built on bracketing parts of ourselves. How often is it based on fully seeing the other side? The test of real resolution of conflict has to do with how much of yourself you bring to the table, and not, as is so often the case, how much of yourself you leave out of who you really are.

In this case we would still see conflict, but we would see it in the context of everything else we share. This was what happened in the series of fights that Becky and I have had over our differing approaches in the ways we have responded to Dini's illness. We have to work hard to refocus our approach to each other so that the conflict, while still there, is set within the larger context of the life we share. We need to remind ourselves that we need each other and our different approaches to be able to deal with Dini's challenges. With all this, we still drive each other up the wall, but we continue to share that wall.

"Bone of my bone and flesh of my flesh." This is how Adam describes Eve. He realizes that this person he will come to love, this woman who will help him discover his deepest desires and realize his greatest capabilities—who will travel with him through the pain of leaving their home in Eden and losing a child—is really a part of him. When he lashes out at her, he will be lashing out at himself as well. When he cares for her and treats her lovingly, he will be nurturing himself at the same time. It's not that they are one and the same, but they are not exactly separate, either.

"What is striking to me," I said to Sarah, "was that you spent all that time in the territories, talking to people, fleshing out a picture of life that was full of injustice and despair. But you didn't report a single conversation in any depth with an Israeli Jew. The people on the other side of the issue you were exploring weren't real to you. They were "unreal" people who were causing "real" pain. What if their pain was as real as yours? What if for every oppression you saw they had experienced an attack, and you had to report that?"

Sarah was a little taken aback. "Everything I wrote was true," she said quickly.

"I know," I said. "But it's like the truth of the four blind men touching an elephant. One, touching the tusk, thinks the elephant is cool and smooth. Another, touching the trunk, thinks it's long and swishy, and so forth. Your truth was total but incomplete. It was one hundred percent correct about fifty percent of the Israeli-Palestinian experience."

Becka's lesson was a little bit different. It was about integrating her ability to continue caring about Israel even if Sarah was right. It was about not walking away from either Israel or her friend because she now had to love an Israel that was imperfect.

I tried to get Becka and Sarah to see that people in Palestine and Israel both love the land. The land is finite, but their love of it is infinite, so of course there is going to be struggle and conflict. It would be so much easier if one side didn't care so much and would just walk away. But the love that we feel for a certain land or a particular set of principles or an understanding of God should not only move us to struggle for what we believe and hold sacred, but soften our hearts for people who feel the same way we do, even if they have reached different conclusions about to whom that land belongs, which set of principles is the one that demands their commitment, or which understanding of God is the one to which they give themselves over. In each case our struggle with them over such issues is triggered not only by what we don't share, but by our common passion for land or values or faith. We don't want to get rid of passion, which is beautiful and makes life worth living. We want to shift our view so that we relate to people differently and realize that what we share is not just conflict. What we share is *love. Ezer k'negdo.*

Adam was deeply lonely, and the being that satisfied his loneliness was also the source of many of his pains and problems. If he had settled for one of the animals as a life partner, something that rabbinic legend imagines as his first approach to his loneliness problem, he would probably never have had the kinds of problems he had with Eve, and he would never have found his life's partner.

It's unlikely that a goat would have engaged the snake in conversation, or that an elephant would have eaten the apple, or that a tiger would have challenged God's command. An independent, strong-willed, unafraid woman did all those things. She was also the only creature capable of having a mature, satisfying relationship that addressed the loneliness that Adam felt.

The mother of my college roommate David, a tiny woman who survived the Holocaust (something about which she never spoke), and one of the most gentle and levelheaded people I have ever met, always said that if you want obedience, get a dog. I try to remember that when my kids are driving me crazy.

The absence of conflict is not the height of relationship. When we feel deeply, conflict is part of the process of loving, and so, too, is the willingness to be there for each other and nurture each other.

We don't need tension in the Middle East to help us see that similarities are particularly susceptible to contention and dispute. Look at virtually any issue that divides the body politic, and you'll see the same principle at work. In the fierce, rancorous debate over abortion, for example, both the pro-life and pro-choice sides share a deep belief in the value of human life and its importance. No pro-choice person is actually saying that there's a little person in the womb who is being murdered and that it's of no consequence. Each side is animated by its desire to protect the life that it sees as affected by an unwanted pregnancy—the mother's in the case of the pro-choice movement, and the baby's in the case of the pro-life movement. That is probably why most people in this country consistently report being both pro-choice and anti-abortion. They appreciate what the most ardent activists for both sides too often fail to see: that holding the truth of both sides at the same time is not only possible, but might actually get us to a healthier debate and better policy around this most divisive of issues.

Two experiences, one with a Planned Parenthood activist, and the other with a hard-core pro-life minister, taught me that failing to see not only where you differ but also where you agree will undermine us every time. When we see the similarities between us, we see new possibilities emerge and new relationships created. We don't lose our identities because of those similarities, but find them more deeply and with greater meaning and sophistication. If all I am is that which you are not, then I have given over control of my identity to you! It is precisely when I can connect to you while maintaining my personal integrity that I find out who I most deeply am.

I was participating in a forum on abortion policy in America and how to bridge the gaps between bitterly divided segments of American society, an event that brought me onto a stage with a leading advocate for Planned Parenthood, a tall woman in a red suit who addressed the audience powerfully and convincingly about the importance of choice as a matter of legal necessity, good health policy, and human dignity. But she started to annoy me when she questioned the motives of anyone who opposed her, claiming that her position was about securing the freedom of all Americans to make choices about their own bodies and lives, not about abortion, and therefore her position was above reproach. That got to me. I don't really think anything is above reproach. That was one of Abraham's life lessons at Sodom: not even God is above reproach. In fact, it's precisely when the things we love most get beyond reproach that they become problematic.

I turned to her and asked her, given her commitment to a woman's right to exercise freedom of choice, when was the last time that she had counseled someone to keep her baby? She froze and then she became quite flustered, asking me why that mattered. It mattered, I responded, because if her position on abortion was really about choice, then both options should be on the table, at least some of the time. So, I persisted, when was the last time she had counseled a young woman to go to term? Never, she admitted. For her, abortion was *not* about choice. In fact, she was very much like the pro-lifers she opposed: each had reached a different conclusion about which action to implement in their respectively choiceless worlds.

The Reverend Michael Bray, perhaps the nation's leading religious voice supporting the murder of doctors who perform abortion, outdid her fanatical pursuit of a preordained conclusion, however. I met with Michael, the author of *A Time to Kill,* which provides the theological underpinnings of such atrocities, in his Ohio home in connection with a documentary about fanaticism on which I was working. Michael welcomed me, suspiciously at first, and then with open arms when he saw that I was not there to embarrass or trap him. I simply wanted to hear, in his own words, how he could live with having inspired people to commit murder.

"It's pretty simple," he said. "It's not murder, it's justice. . . . I am simply trying to do everything in my power to protect those innocent little babies."

"But what about the families of those 'guilty' doctors over whose death you lose no sleep?" I asked. "What would you say to the wife and children of people like Barnett Slepian, the physician who was shot down in his own living room by a sniper with a high-powered hunting rifle?" There was an uncomfortable silence, and I continued, "Michael, please tell me that you have a teaching that reconciles your agony over the loss of those babies, an agony that I believe is deep, sincere, and with which I find a measure of sympathy, and your willingness to actually celebrate the death of Dr. Slepian."

"Well," he argued, "some death is ordained and some is not."

"In which case," I said to him, "you are just like Dr. Slepian.

You have reached a definitive conclusion about who should live and who should die. It may be that the two decisions are not the same, it may be that one is right and the other is wrong, but it is certain that those deciding are more alike than either recognizes or admits. If they could, perhaps, reconcile and admit that, then the nature of the debate would shift from vilification and denigration to passionate but peaceful disagreement, and fewer doctors would die."

The pro-choice people portray the pro-life people as hateful misogynists, but the pro-lifers actually believe that abortion is tantamount to capital punishment. Both sides believe in the sanctity of life and the dignity of human beings. Disagreements can arise over quality of life versus quantity of life. For example, if my fetus has a horrible birth defect, can I terminate pregnancy? Again, on both sides of this question will be people who care about life. Both sides are trying to balance the same concerns. One side is measuring the quality of life that the person might have as he or she travels through life with an especially heavy burden. The other side sees the quantity of life that each of us represents as so profound that it compensates for the perceived compromise in quality of life. In each case, life is at the center. That is why the two sides debate each other with such vigor: they are actually two sides of the same coin. It is precisely because they are so close that the fight is so intense.

We care about things that are close to us, not far from us. The people with whom we have the most painful and difficult disagreements are often closer to our position and point of view than we can imagine. If we could recognize that instead of only focusing on our difference, then the way we fight, how long we fight, even why we fight might change.

It's not that everything would be instantly better. *Ezer k'nedgo,* "a helper against him," guarantees that there will be strife—that is part of growth, intimacy, caring, and family. What we are yearning for is to be able to tap into the deep well of human wisdom that our collective history and religious traditions are capable of providing, and finding a way to reach out and become more; to reach out and take chances with other people who are different, whom we are afraid of or alienated from. From whom we are disconnected.

Just because you have a crazy uncle Eddie that you don't get along with doesn't mean that you should deny him a seat at your table at family gatherings. The whole of our human family belongs at the table. You don't have to sit next to Uncle Eddie. You don't have to schmooze him all night. He can be seated next to someone else who gets along better with him than you do. What matters is that he is included—that he is at the table.

A dam and Eve were not the Cosbys. And Becky and I were not and are not the Cosbys, either, as we butt heads over the challenges of parenting Dini, or Avi and Dassi, or a million other things. Adam and Eve's relationship—like all enduring, lasting unions—had its struggles and conflicts. But what if we could hold inside ourselves that the "helper who is against us" may also be our greatest ally? I think that would change the nature of our struggles, if not in the world, then at least in our own families; and if not in our own families, then at least in our own hearts.

Adam and Eve are the models for our larger web of human connection. They were not Jews, Christians, Muslims, or Hindus. They were not from any particular nation or tribe. They are the common ancestors we all share. That is why their story belongs to all of us, no matter what tradition we claim as our own. Every other ancient creation story begins with the founding of the tribe and tells that particular story. It tells the story that explains why that people is the best people, why its land is the best land, or why its god loves it over all other peoples. Not this one. Although the story of Adam and Eve is preserved in the Hebrew Bible, it is not the story of the first Jews. That story would wait for twenty generations and twelve chapters in the Book of Genesis, and even then as we follow the saga of the Jewish people, beginning with Abraham, it is clear that we have merely shifted our attention to a single test case in the grand experiment called human history.

The message is clear. To be Jewish is just one subset of what it is to be human, as is the case with every other race and ethnicity. We are all part of the same family. I fear that I sound like an advertisement for the Small World ride at Disneyland, or the newest episode of *Barney*. But that lesson in Genesis flows from two people who lead tumultuous, conflict-ridden lives. Adam and Eve's story is filled with bumps and bruises and pain. But along the way it reminds us that, ultimately, we all share the same ancestors, the same beginning, and we are all on this journey together.

CHAPTER NINE

A Person's a Person, No Matter How Small

Talking About the Things That Matter

Most in the Way That Hurts the Least

THE ISLAMIC HOUSE OF WISDOM IS LOCATED IN DEARBORN, Michigan, a suburb of Detroit. When you walk down the street, virtually every other sign is in Arabic or Farsi, advertising hallal meat and discount fares to Mecca. It doesn't look so different from my neighborhood of Riverdale, a section of the Bronx in New York City, with its concentration of modern orthodox Jews, except that in my neighborhood the signs are for kosher meat and airfare to Tel Aviv. To most people these differences are insignificant details, evidence of life in two similarly exotic ethnic communities. Mecca and Tel Aviv are only a few hundred miles apart; the laws of hallal and kosher are closely related. But for the Muslims and Jews living in Riverdale and Dearborn, those details make a world of difference. As I walked down the street, I was acutely aware of how the degrees of similarity and of difference were paradoxically and simultaneously true.

I had come to Dearborn and the Islamic House of Wisdom to attend the premiere of a television series that I had created called *Building Bridges: Abrahamic Perspectives on the World Today* for Bridges TV, the American Muslim network based in Buffalo, New York. The show is a weekly roundtable with different imams, priests, ministers, and me discussing the issues of the day. We discuss everything from the war in Iraq to displaying the Ten Commandments in schools and courthouses. We have focused on the challenge of raising spiritually connected kids, and the reality of interfaith families. Basically, if it matters, we talk about it. We try to use the wisdom of our faiths to find spiritual solutions to contemporary problems and demonstrate that disagreement doesn't always have to be about demonizing the people with whom we disagree.

Mo Hassan and Aasiya Zubair, a Pakistani couple, are almost regal in their bearing. Both are unusually tall and project the kind of strength and intensity that I've noticed often characterizes successful entrepreneurs. Before he founded the network, Mo was a banker, and Aasiya was busy raising their four kids. Then came 9/11. The network was their response.

As a result of 9/11 and many events since, walls are going up all over the world. That is understandable, even necessary. But at precisely the moment when we put up the most walls, we need to make sure that we put in some windows, and perhaps even some doors. Hassan and Zubair knew Americans needed a way to learn about the American Muslim community without having to visit a mosque, and American Muslims needed a place through which millions of them could be reached by the larger American public.

Hassan and Zubair have outdone my *bubbe* in Palm Springs. She only intuited that being in America could actually fulfill a whole set of ancient Jewish values, which is why she was always proud of being Jewish, but deeply suspicious of religious tradition. Hassan and Zubair believe that for immigrant Muslims, being in America is not just about hunkering down, making money, and hoping to get back to the old country unscathed. They are committed to creating something new: a spiritual identity that is both genuinely Islamic and deeply American. They want to help the six million Muslims in America open up to the experience of America and help Americans open up to the Muslims in their midst—a process that will be mutually beneficial, just as it was for Jews like my great-grandparents, who were both affected by this country and helped make it into what it is today.

One of the people the station wanted me to invite to be a panelist on the show was an Iranian imam, Mohammed Ali Elahi, who heads the Islamic House of Wisdom. Elahi had been a chaplain in the Iranian navy, a post with overt political overtones since there is no one working in Iran's armed forces who isn't proud of the ayatollahs. Elahi has publicly said that Iran's president is misunderstood, Hamas is not a terrorist organization, and the world has nothing to fear from Iran having nuclear weapons—and that is only the beginning of the things about which we disagree. But that is precisely why I was open to having him on the show. It is most important to talk with those people with whom we most disagree.

Of course, there are limits to this openness, as I found

out when I was invited last year to a breakfast with President Ahmadinejad of Iran, organized for some twenty American religious leaders. I simply could not go, but not because I think that anyone should be excluded from being a possible partner in conversation. I knew that I would simply not be able to get past my own anger at him to participate in the conversation constructively. I am angry at him because he denies that the Holocaust occurred, calls for the violent destruction of Israel, and invokes the kind of triumphalist apocalyptic philosophy that really can get us all killed. Not to mention that because he holds all of these positions, it makes it impossible to explore and even learn from his remarkable ability to see the dark underbelly of our own excesses, which he sees as far greater than they are, but which we ignore at our peril. I also didn't want to go to the breakfast because it was likely to be used as political propaganda by the Iranians. I would love to spend a few hours in private conversation with President Ahmadinejad because he is a fascinating leader who merges politics and religion in powerful new ways.

With Elahi, there was no evidence that he was looking to exploit his participation in the show as a sign of my approval of his views. He is the imam of the second-largest Shia mosque in Detroit, and, given his prominence, although I may disagree with him, it would be foolish to discount him. The limits of whom we talk with and whom we don't should be a function of our ability to remain constructive in the conversation, not simply the degree to which the other person with whom we want to speak already agrees with us. This is true both among religious leaders and in our personal lives. We retain both the power and the responsibility to determine with whom we talk and under what circumstances—which is something that I try to be mindful of when I yell at Becky or the girls that it's impossible to talk with them. That may be true, but that's because of who I am at that moment at least as much as because of who they are.

The decision to have Imam Elahi on my show, not to mention view its premiere from his mosque, had created an uproar. I was called to task by both Jewish organizations and general political groups. "You can't talk to him," I was told. "He says terrible things." I was told that I "would be punished" if I went ahead and appeared in public with him, and my career would be in jeopardy. People would see to it that I "would be finished in Jewish life." I was called a traitor. My love of Israel was questioned, along with my commitment to the Jewish community. I was shocked. I began to realize that my "sin" lay in the claim that disagreement was no excuse for not talking. I had touched that raw nerve, that insidious reflex that says you *do* have to be wrong for me to be right.

My response was that these groups could, and probably should, boycott the show. In a sophisticated pluralistic community there will be some people who will just say, "I want no part of this; count me out." That's fine. In fact, those people play a very important role as border guards who help ensure the integrity and security of the community. But all borders have to have gates; otherwise they imprison those within as much as they keep perceived danger away. Some people are better at guarding the gates, and others are better at scouting the territory beyond them. We always need both kinds of people, and at different times in our lives we need to draw on each of those approaches.

We taped the shows in which Elahi appeared in October of

2006, and I thought they worked out well. We were able to really talk to each other, although we often disagreed. I was able to push him on the dangers of his belief that the absolute truth was knowable entirely through his own understanding of Islam without offending him, although, to be honest, I think that I came close to alienating him on more than one occasion. He was willing to challenge my understanding of faith because it left room for so many questions.

Given our profound disagreement about so many big issues, I felt it was an amazing and wonderful thing that Elahi was going to let me stand in his pulpit, address his community, and introduce *Bridges* on the night of its premiere. I flew in from New York, gave a series of interviews from my room at the Red Roof Inn for radio programs that were interested in the show, and then hopped in a white rental car to drive over to the Islamic House of Wisdom.

It was a winter night in the suburbs of Motor City, and I was not all that far from Birmingham, where my *bubbe* and her husband, Sam, had ultimately settled in what had been, until their arrival, a restricted community, one into which they bought their way with proceeds from my great-grandfather's real estate and hotel businesses that had earned him a place in the book *Men Who Made Michigan,* of which he was so proud. The irony was not lost on me. Here I was, in the city where my own family had begun to find its place in America four generations ago, trying to complete that process by finding my own place, one that was simultaneously more particularly Jewish than was theirs, and also more overtly connected to members of other faith communities.

Any illusions about the great success that the premiere of

the show was going to have were shattered when we pulled up into the parking lot of the mosque, a huge building that had been converted from what had been an old Assemblies of God church, the charismatic form of evangelical Christianity that produced the Reverend Jimmy Swaggart and Jerry Lee Lewis. The mosque had bought the building and put a dome on top of its flat roof and a minaret on top of the dome. The prayer hall easily has space for a thousand people, and there is a huge parking lot attached to the building—which was mostly empty when I arrived. Frankly, I was rattled. It seemed that Jews and Muslims had finally found common ground in rejecting what suddenly felt like a misguided attempt to find common ground! Then I realized that we were making history. This event wasn't even supposed to happen, this show was not supposed to be made, but it did and it was, and while it would have been nice to have a large audience that night, we had an audience of at least hundreds of thousands in living rooms across the country, living rooms in which no such conversations as the ones that Elahi and I had would be aired.

The imam greeted me in the entrance to the mosque, wearing a broad smile and dressed in a beautiful gown and turban. We walked into the mosque's very large hall in which the rather small audience had gathered, and I realized that for him this was a great success because the event was happening and he had helped make it happen without losing the support of his community. And he knew we were proving to the world that such exchanges *could* happen.

I now realize that the premiere was a success on those terms, and that I should not have been seduced by the easy affirmation that comes from having a large audience. I had to trust for myself the very same markers of success that I acknowledged for Elahi.

The premiere was one of those learning moments in which I was reminded that success was largely a matter of expectations. The moment I stopped worrying about the crowd and focused on the fact that we had pulled off an unprecedented encounter, one that demonstrated the richness of talking to those people "with whom we cannot talk," I relaxed. I was led to the stage and seated next to the imam's seat. He went right to the pulpit, from which he offered a brief prayer and a word of welcome, and then invited me to introduce the evening. I thanked the audience for their warm welcome, for their willingness to hold the event in their sanctuary, and for inviting me to explain what the show was all about. What the show was about, I said, was a very simple teaching of the rabbis, having to do with the meaning of wisdom that guides so much of this work. "Who is wise?" the rabbis ask. The one who learns from every person, they answer. Not about what they already believe, or from those people with whom they largely agree—but from every person. I told the small group that had gathered in the House of Wisdom that night that this was why I had come to Detroit—to celebrate this teaching, and I had made this show to share that insight of the rabbis with as many people as possible. My presence in that room was about acknowledging that I had things to learn from Mohammed Ali Elahi and, frankly, to evoke in him the awareness that he had things to learn from me.

I had wanted to share this particular teaching in Elahi's mosque because of what had happened one day during the taping of the show in Buffalo. Elahi had taken me aside. It quickly became clear that he wanted to talk Middle East politics, and I knew I was in for an exchange that would be difficult at best. Although I have witnessed some of the more problematic elements of Israel's policies firsthand, I believe in Israel's right to exist, the fact that the Jewish people should not be the only ethnic-religious community without a national home. While all human loss is equally painful to those who mourn, the circumstances of such loss are not morally equal. I acknowledge that when a suicide bomber dies, his parents may be in no less pain than the parents of his victims, but that does not mean I do not distinguish between the fact that one was the perpetrator of a crime and the others are his victims. My ability to mourn does not take away my ability to judge, but neither does my ability to judge give me an excuse to close my eyes to the pain that everyone touched by such an act can feel.

Quickly the conversation took the turn I feared. Elahi became strident and launched into a stream of invective about how the real terrorist in the Middle East is Israel, that Israel is an artificial nation mercilessly imposed on the entire Muslim community, and that Zionism itself is a perversion of the shared values of humanity, including what he called the best values found within Jewish tradition.

I finally had to stop him. "I don't think anything you've said is true," I said. "But I still want to take you seriously because I know that your views are held sincerely and that your desire is not to hurt me, correct?"

"Of course," he replied, calming down a bit. "But I am right."

"Let's assume you are right," I said. "I can't hear you when you talk to me that way, and neither can anyone else in my community that doesn't already agree with you. For your own sake, for the purpose of being more effective at getting your own message out, can you find a way to make your case so that it doesn't make me feel completely wrong as soon as you open your mouth? Because if you can do that, I'll hear you better and listen more closely to what you are saying."

Elahi was stunned. I'm not sure if that was because I wasn't interested in playing his game of "which side is right," or because I really was interested in hearing him out, although we both knew there was little chance that he would convince me of his position. From that point on the conversation engaged me intensely. We had grown to respect each other during the taping of the show. I was hearing a highly intelligent, intensely passionate presentation of ideas that I knew existed, but I had never heard from someone about whom I personally cared in quite that way.

There is a beautiful story from the Talmud that lays out seven steps that show us how to help make such conversations happen, to live a life of knowing that someone else doesn't always have to be wrong for you to be right. This technique helps us see that even if people are wrong about one thing, they don't have to be wrong about everything, and that we really can sustain relationships through profound disagreements, at least more often than we usually do. And finally, given that we all have our breaking point, in the moments when we really do need to walk away, we can do so in a way that makes it more likely that we will come back together at some point in the future.

The seven steps teach us how to have those conversations that are potentially the most hurtful—usually the ones we most need to have but never seem to, either because we are afraid that we will get hurt by them or that we will become hurtful to others in the midst of them. The rabbis spent hundreds of years arguing and fighting with each other, but it didn't keep them from coming back to the table and continuing the conversation. They were able to do that because of these seven steps, which liberate us to bring to the surface our real disagreements, even take strong action in light of them, but do so in a way that makes it possible to maintain the dignity of all those involved and the promise of healing the wounds that are always a part of any relationship about which we really care.

The story in the Talmud that leads to the seven steps begins with a seemingly tiny detail—the legal status of a *tanoor,* a beehive-shaped cooking oven (not unlike a tandoori oven in Indian restaurants) that was built from clay tiles, when one of those tiles becomes impure, perhaps because it has come in contact with a dead body.

Like the differences between Dearborn and Riverdale, little differences—like one impure tile—can make a world of difference. Show me a person who says that no details matter and I'll show you a person who doesn't really care about anything at all. It is vital, however, to realize that no one set of details is the right set, while all others are ridiculous. We need to remember that one person's sacred details are another person's obsessive compulsive disorder. Or, if you prefer spiritual language, the devil is in the details—but so is God. That's why people fight about which end of the toothpaste their partners squeeze, and whether or not the toilet seat is left up or down. That's why it bothers me that after twenty years of asking Becky to give me a glass of water or soda, and even though we have big, beautiful twenty-ounce glasses, she never puts more than twelve ounces in. Why can't she just fill the glass up? Of course, I'd have to be some kind of idiot to let that annoy me; after all, she's my best friend, a great wife, and a wonderful mother, not to mention that I can always get my own stupid drink if I don't like the way she fills my glass.

All this is true, and yet it is in little details like these that we have the chance to really demonstrate our care and concern for each other, for not only doing what someone wants, but for doing it in a way that works for them. Sometimes that involves how we fill a glass for our partner, whether we twist a turban right or left before we enter a temple, or how we judge the implications of a single impure tile in a *tanoor*.

That kind of sensitivity to detail, to the "small stuff," is beautiful; it's the basis of my kids' favorite Dr. Seuss book, *Horton Hears a Who*. In the book, Horton the elephant can hear the sounds coming from a speck of dust, and he figures out that there is an entire community living in that dust speck. None of the other animals in the jungle can hear the sounds coming from the speck, and they mock his concern when they blow on the flower upon which the speck rests because Horton says they are endangering Whoville, the place on the speck where the Whos live. Horton tells all the Whos to make noise, so much noise that the other animals will hear them. They scream and shout to no avail until they discover one little Who who is not doing his part. When that little Who adds his voice to the general clamor, the Whos suddenly become audible to all the other animals, because, as the book's refrain states, "A person's a person, no matter how small."

Horton shows us that little things matter. It can be a speck of dust or a little Who or one impure tile that means the whole oven will have to be destroyed and rebuilt, a ruling that would have implications for the Jewish community and would impose economic hardship on a potentially large number of people. The debate about the impure tile wasn't just academic.

Eventually, most of the rabbis ruled that if one of the tiles was impure, then the entire oven should be considered impure and should not be used. One rabbi named Eliezer, however, said that a single tile could not make an entire oven impure, because any one tile could be separated from the oven and therefore should not be considered an integral part of it.

If one tile is impure, all are impure, argued the majority against Eliezer. The majority felt that the notion of interconnectedness was so powerful that they could not simply overlook the hassles and hardship that came with it. That's how it is with most people who focus on and are attached to details. They are not trying to be difficult; they have only located meaning in the details that the rest of us don't see or that simply don't matter to us.

When we see fanatics and religious zealots decrying the state of the world, venting their anger and rage at the "impurities" that are brought about by people who do not think and act as they do, it might be useful to try to see that they must feel very connected to the world, otherwise they wouldn't care. The

people who are screaming their heads off feel deeply connected
to those about whom they are screaming. After all, it would be
far easier for them to sit back and watch the rest of us destroy
ourselves while they wait for God to carry them off to whatever
heaven they believe in. It is almost as if fanaticism were a cancerous manifestation of the feeling of connection. The same thing
that makes us care about people we don't even know, done right,
means that when they hurt, we hurt; done wrong, it means that
when they don't feel what we're feeling, we kill them.

The argument that we should simply live and let live is as
dangerous when brought to its logical extreme as the notion of
connection that has become cancerous because it invades everything. In fact, if overbearing connectedness can be compared to
a cancer growing out of control, then limitless live and let live
can be compared to amputation, in which the outcome is an
array of disconnected limbs.

Ultimately, Eliezer lost the argument with his colleagues,
but not before working a series of miracles designed to show
that God was on his side. He made trees jump, streams flow
backward, and walls fall down. In his final gambit, he said, "If
I'm right, let Heaven prove it." And a voice from on high replies,
"What's your problem? Eliezer is always right."

Rabbi Joshua responded that the dispute wasn't for God to
decide. Right or wrong, it was a dispute that had to be settled
among the rabbis, here on earth. Later generations of sages
wondered how God took being reminded that it was time to
butt out. They asked the prophet Elijah, who shows up in Jewish
legends written long after the time of the Bible as a carrier of
messages between heaven and earth. Elijah responded that God

laughed and said, "My children have defeated me." A better translation would be, "My children have outdone me." Or, "My children have made me eternal." Only when children can take real responsibility for themselves can parents know that they will live eternally through their children and their children's children.

And beyond that sense of immortality, isn't that what all good parents want? We want our children to be independent, to be able to stand on their own two feet and make their own decisions. We want our kids to be better human beings and more fulfilled than we are. We want their lives to be richer and more rewarding than ours have been. There is joy in seeing them go beyond us, beyond what we even thought was possible.

In a world where people really do take power and exercise their creative capacities, there will always be conflicts, like those between parents and children, husbands and wives, and Eliezer and the rest of the rabbinic council. The rabbis, who recognized that conflict was a healthy part of human relationships, developed seven steps to deal with conflict in a constructive way that neither diminishes our freedom to differ nor encourages us to demolish those who oppose us.

The first step, said the rabbis, is to admit that sometimes you need a break, that not everybody always has to be together for every conversation, and that it can even be appropriate to tell some people that they are not welcome to participate in yours. And that is precisely what Rabbi Eliezer's colleagues did to him: they excommunicated him. They took a vote and decided that their esteemed colleague needed a time-out. That's exactly what

it was. It was not an eternal judgment rendered against someone for a single act that would permanently cut him off from his
community. That power is unique to God: infinite power is best
kept in the hands of an infinite being.

The rabbis excommunicated Eliezer for thirty days. Imagine if the framework in which we conducted our harshest as-
sessments of those with whom we most deeply disagreed came
with the requirement that we would revisit our assessment each
thirty days. Would we necessarily come back together at the end
of the month? No, but it would sure keep us from letting the in-
ertia of not being together become an excuse for not at least trying to work things out.

Step two, the rabbis show us, demands that we never lose
sight of the basic dignity of even the worst person in our midst.
Having concluded that excommunication is the way to go, the
rabbis asked themselves, Who's going to go tell Eliezer that he
needs a time-out? Eliezer's closest friend, Rabbi Akiva, volun-
teered, saying, "I'll go, because if someone else tells him the
wrong way, it will destroy an entire world." That's how valuable
even the most difficult character in our midst must always be,
and it's the lesson of step two. Even when we are doing the right
thing, if we don't do it with respect for those against whom we
act, we'll destroy more than we accomplish.

That awareness leads to step three: radical empathy. Akiva
dresses in black clothes and sits no closer than six feet to Eliezer,
acting as if he, Akiva, were the one who was excommunicated.
He lives the lesson that until we are willing ourselves to experience the pain of being put outside the circle, we have no moral
authority to impose that experience on others.

Eliezer, realizing that something serious has happened, says, "Akiva, what's going on?"

"Master," Akiva replies, "it appears that we have to distance ourselves from you."

Akiva is reminding Eliezer, and us, that even during this time-out, Eliezer retains his power, his wholeness, his dignity, the respect of his friends and community, his position as "master." The fact that someone has done one wrong thing can never invalidate all the other things he has done right. Only when we are willing to recognize that can we impose a sanction on them for specific transgressions. Even when a punishment is required, it is designed to change a specific behavior or attitude, not to strip a person of his or her power or independence, or to change who he or she is. And the Talmud says that whenever Eliezer looked at anything, it burned up. Even having been excommunicated, he still had power. His dignity and power were preserved. We need to figure out how the person who we can't bear at any given moment, from whom we need to distance ourselves, remains our teacher and retains his power, dignity, and authority. Figuring that out is step four.

Having heard himself addressed as master, Eliezer submits. He sits on the ground, wears black clothes, and gives in to the will of the council. But even though the sanction of Eliezer has been carried out in the most caring, compassionate way possible, the Talmud teaches us that at precisely the moment when Eliezer's sentence was imposed, one-third of the crops in the land shriveled up and died. This is step five: acknowledging that there are always consequences when we are engaged in conflict. Even when everything is done right, there is a price to be paid. It will always cost us when other people are hurt even by our "just" or right action—and we must never pretend otherwise.

That's where the story ends for Eliezer, but not for us. The rabbi who had headed the court that presided over this entire dispute, Gamliel, was traveling on a ship some time later, when huge waves rose out of the sea, threatening to capsize the boat and drown him. "This must be because of what we did to Rabbi Eliezer," Gamliel says. The right thing was done the right way, and yet the first thing to come into Gamliel's mind was his own accountability. That is step six: accountability for what is going wrong that begins with you and not with the other guy. That was what my father was teaching me by pointing a thumb at himself rather than a finger at someone else. Even when you are right, you can be wrong. Step six is a corollary of step four, which tells us that even when someone is wrong, they have things to teach us.

Recognizing that fact leads to step seven, which is the guiding principle of this approach to conflict. Gamliel says, "God, you know I didn't do this to Eliezer for myself or for my father or family. I did it for your honor, God." The waves persist, washing over the gunwales of Gamliel's boat and threatening to capsize the boat and drown him. All the excuses Gamliel offered are so easily abused. The only thing worse than acting for ego and family honor is acting for God. And God knows that. Then Gamliel cries out, "I did what I did so there wouldn't be strife in the community. I acted against Rabbi Eliezer only so we could be together, so that we could continue to grow and argue and accept the freedom that you have given us." Then, suddenly, the waves subsided. Because in the end the only justification for censure, even when it's done carefully and ethically and sensitively, is to allow the greatest number of us—a couple or a nation or the whole world—to hang together. If those relationships don't remain more important than the ideas over which we fight, than we shouldn't be fighting. However important ideas and beliefs may be, people are more important. And whatever tradition knows and can transmit, that will settle the seas and calm the waves.

This was exactly what I was trying to say to Imam Elahi in our painful and contentious discussion of politics in the Middle East. I wanted him to know that beyond any areas of disagreement, it was our relationship and connection that was what was most important to me. I wanted us to find a way to speak to each other about our profound differences that made it more likely than not that we would continue our conversation, because whether or not we liked what the other had to say, we would recognize and be open to the fact that we both had things to learn from each other.

We need to enter into difficult and painful conversations knowing that we will be challenged and stretched. That is really how we grow. But it has to be safe to enter into such conversations, and that safety is guaranteed by the pledge that we make to follow the seven steps, or something like them. We need a way to talk to one another that guarantees that we put the dignity of the person in front of us before the correctness of our own ideas.

Only then will we be able to see that we can remain open while still maintaining the integrity of our beliefs. It's a difficult but rewarding balancing act, one that was useful and vital in Talmudic times and is desperately needed today. We can learn from the wisdom of the sages how we can listen and learn and empathize without losing sight of who we are, what we care about, and what matters most to us, down to the last niggling, irrelevant detail, which, like Whoville, may contain a whole world.

CHAPTER TEN

THE FOOTPRINTS OF
THE MESSIAH

Turning Our Deepest Dreams into

an Everyday Reality

M ICHELLE MARTIN OF ABC'S *NIGHTLINE* INTERVIEWED ME
for a show that aired during Christmas week in 2004.
Much of what I talked about with her contributed to the thinking that was the genesis of this book.

"Don't people think you're too idealistic?" she asked me.

"If religion and spirit and faith don't make you idealistic,
what's the point?" I responded. "That doesn't mean that I'm
naïve, which is a very dangerous thing to be in this world."

"What's the difference between naïveté and idealism?"
she said.

I explained that idealism recognizes the difference between how things are and how they could be, and it expects us
to get to that better place, or at least to move continually in that

direction. I don't know exactly how long that will take or what the exact steps should be, and I know that there will be false stops and starts. But to be idealistic is to believe that life holds more potential than we can possibly imagine, and that much of that potential will eventually be realized.

Naïveté says we're already there, it's fine, we've arrived. It smacks of an arrogant certainty that we will achieve all that we hope for by means that we already possess. I don't know. Perhaps all of this is just the splitting of philosophical hairs. I just know that is not how I want to live. I want horizons that are big, and the freedom to fail to achieve things I want, without feeling that I have failed in my life.

As I look back on it, I think what Michelle was really asking me was, "Can we really allow ourselves to go through life with this approach? Do we make ourselves vulnerable? We open ourselves up to disappointment, and to the genuine pain that comes with it. We build up expectations of ourselves and of others in our lives, and they don't always pan out. But, as the Kabbalists of Safed wrote five hundred years ago, the final deed begins with the first thought. We can only do what we first imagine. I don't think it's deluded to dare to live not only in light of how things are, but how they might be, as long as we remember that there is a gap between our ideals and reality, and we attend to that reality even as we seek to enhance it. As I was waiting nervously to see if I would be awarded a major fellowship, my mentor in graduate school, Professor Shaye J. D. Cohen, told me that I should hope for the best but plan for the worst. It was good advice then, and it is good advice now. We need to have horizons that are bigger than reality; we need unreasonable, soaring aspirations. That's what it means to be journeying toward the land I will show you. To seek is to keep moving, to keep hoping, to keep faith.

That same professor who told me to hope for the best but plan for the worst once described how he went through the apartment of his mentor, Morton Smith, a professor of ancient history at Columbia University, after Smith had passed away. Smith's desk was filled with notes for ideas that he hadn't found time to develop, and reflections on ideas that he had come to see as misguided. Shaye remarked that that was exactly how he hoped they would find his study one day. Far from being a sign of failure, of a life left incomplete, that kind of desk marks a life that was lived with horizons that were bigger than reality could hold, a life that aspired to more than turned out to be possible. That is the journey through the desert that wanders, in the words of Genesis, "back and forth." Far from being a failure, that is a real marker of success.

For me, idealism is part of faith, or perhaps faith is the ultimate expression of idealism. Vaclav Havel, the playwright and former president of the Czech Republic, wrote beautifully about the spiritual affinity of faith, idealism, and hope: "Hope . . . is a dimension of the soul. It is an orientation of the spirit, an orientation of the heart; it transcends the world that is immediately experienced, and is anchored somewhere beyond its horizons. . . . Hope, in this deep and powerful sense, is not the same as joy that things are going well. . . . Hope is definitely not the same thing as optimism. It is not the conviction that something will turn out well, but the certainty that something makes sense, regardless of how well it turns out."

Havel's "orientation of the spirit" is the needle of the compass that guides our lives. It sets Abraham on his journey as a seeker. That journey continues, even as Abraham buys land in Hebron that includes the Cave of Makhpelah, the tomb for Sarah, his wife, the helper who is against him. His death does not mark the end of his story or his journey. Another story begins—that of the generations that came after him and the three faiths that he fathered. His story continues in every one of us.

Does that mean we will be doomed to endless wandering? That we will never arrive? If so, what is at the root of faith? It's often thought that the end of that journey is the coming of the Messiah—a person, man or woman, who will appear and redeem the world. Whether the Messiah is known as Mashiach, Messiah, Mahdi, the anointed one, or "he who has risen," our faiths all look forward to a leader who will usher in a time of peace and wholeness for all humanity. Some people believe that he has yet to appear, while others insist that he has appeared and will return to finish the work that he has started. Many are uncomfortable with the term or idea of the Messiah, period. But whether or not we believe in the Messiah, we can share in the aspiration for a better world.

Tell me your dreams, your messianic vision, and I will tell you about the reality that you're creating. I know what it is like to yearn for the end of the story, for closure and completion, peace and wholeness and the certainty that you have arrived and no longer need to struggle.

The coming of the Messiah was often in my heart and in my thoughts as my fellow settlers and I danced through the streets of Hebron, a handful of Jews possessed by an ecstatic vision of redemption, of return, of a promise long delayed but not forgotten. We were bringing an ancient prophecy to life: that we Jews would return to the land of Israel and reclaim our birthright. Against all odds, we were doing just that. If we could return to Israel after thousands of years, we truly believed that anything was possible. Why not a world without sickness, war, or even death! We were dancing after the footsteps of the Messiah.

I know it may sound foolish to some of you, but I do not believe I was following the footsteps of the Pied Piper. The glowing footprints that led me on *were* the Messiah's, just as when we walk into Sloan-Kettering and see the work that brilliant minds are doing to cheat death, we behold a place where the Messiah walks. In each case, we see a willingness to live and work as if we could turn our most deeply held dreams into everyday reality. Our failure in Hebron lay in failing to admit how others were forced to pay the price of that process, much as it would be to use cancer patients in Sloan-Kettering as experimental subjects without their permission.

But, if done properly, each of those experiments is nothing short of messianic, drawing on a tradition that says that as much as the world depends on the Messiah to make the world whole again, the Messiah depends on us to allow that redemption to happen. Behind this teaching is profound appreciation of every human being's potential for greatness, for playing a part in creating the world in which we all long to live.

This teaching is behind the circumcision ceremony in traditional Judaism that each male infant undergoes when he is eight days old. The baby is placed in what we call "Elijah's chair," because in Jewish tradition it is Elijah the prophet who announces the coming of the Messiah. By putting the child in that chair, we're saying that maybe this child is the one. That tradition has been expanded in many Jewish communities so that daughters are placed in Elijah's chair during naming ceremonies because maybe the Messiah is female.

The same power contained in this ceremony is found in the story of an unknown woman giving birth to an infant in a manger in what can only be described as having been a back-water village south of Jerusalem, a young man who embodies God's presence on earth and offers himself to carry our pain and bring us closer to God.

That same power is found in another story of a young man of limited education and few prospects who was chosen by God to bring a new revelation to the world from out of the deserts of Arabia. In each case the infant in Elijah's chair or the Christ-child in the manger, or the emergence of the prophet Muhammad, the stories hint at the possibility that if it could be them, then it could be any of us.

Imagine how we would treat every child in the world if we believed each one might be the Messiah. Would we let children live in unspeakable poverty in this, the richest country in the world, or starve in Africa, or be blown up on their way to pre-school in Baghdad?

This tradition expressed the ancient rabbis' deep reverence for every human life. It reflects the first fact of human existence in the Book of Genesis—that every human being is created in the image of the divine. What does that mean? The rabbis distilled their response to that question down to three things.

The first is that each of us is of infinite value. That's

where the oft-quoted teaching springs from that if you save one person you save a whole world, and when you lose one person you lose a whole world. Imagine how it would be if we really appreciated each other in that way. What if we looked at each person as the last precious example of a species that would die when he or she died?

This is part of the second characteristic that the rabbis taught: each person is unique. It's not true with human beings that if you've seen one person you've seen them all. Actually the opposite is true: each person you encounter—when you see in this way—fuels your desire to engage with other human beings and to better understand each of them because you know that while we are all related, each one of us is unique.

The third thing that the rabbis teach is that while each of us is unique, all of us are equal. Of course, balancing the equal claims of infinitely important people is not so easy; ask any loving parent. But as I say to my kids all the time (and the fact that I say it all the time simply means that it's a hard lesson for all of us, both to learn and to teach): equality is not about everybody getting the same thing, but about everybody getting what he or she needs, and that those needs are equally important.

There is a story in the Talmud that illustrates this point. A poor man appears before the alms council for aid. He explains to them that he was once a rich man, and that he owned a coach with fine horses and footmen in uniform who ran alongside it. "I would very much like to have that coach and footmen again," he says to the rabbis. "Can you help me?"

Our first response may be, "How ridiculous! The arrogance of some people!" But in the story, the sage Hillel is willing to ask the council to buy the coach for the man. Why? Because in an ideal world, each of us is entitled to that which makes him feel whole.

As a practice, take a moment to imagine that somehow the person you love most and the person you hate most are fundamentally equal. Perhaps you're having trouble conjuring someone you truly hate. Well, imagine that someone is attacking you and wants to kill you. Imagine that they've shot at you first. You're shooting back. Imagine that you feel totally justified when you pull the trigger. You're totally convinced that you're doing the right thing, in the right way, at the right time. Now imagine that your bullet finds its intended target. Further imagine that somewhere that night a mother and father and maybe sisters and brothers and perhaps even the children of the person you have killed are experiencing you as a murderer.

It doesn't matter that you're totally justified in your actions. The loss of the people who loved the person you've killed is real. They've lost a world, and it doesn't matter what the context is. That doesn't mean you don't fight that fight. But it does mean that while you can go home thinking that you've done the right thing, for someone else you're a murderer. That realization may well lead to seeing alternative responses to that very situation the next time around, or even constructing a reality in which fewer people face that situation.

This is not just an arbitrary exercise. For example, I opened fire when the bus from Hebron to Jerusalem on which I was riding one Saturday night was attacked. We were outside of a Palestinian refugee camp near Bethlehem when burning tires came rolling at us and we realized that we were being shot at. I don't know if my bullets found their mark.

I don't regret my actions, but I do try to keep my heart open to the pain I may have caused. Of course, some of you will feel that it was the fault of all those on the bus for being there as unwanted occupiers to begin with. Others will doubtless see me as soft and deluded for agonizing twenty-four years later about what was clearly a case of self-defense. But what I hope each of you, no matter which side of that debate you're on, will share with me is the awareness that the lives endangered that night were *all* sacred and that it was a sad night for the human race. When we can recognize and acknowledge that sadness, we might have fewer such nights, even if we continue to disagree about who was right and who was wrong. That's what it means to keep faith with your people and your politics without becoming a fanatic. That is what it means for ideas to matter, but for human relations to matter more. That is when we hear the footsteps of the Messiah.

It doesn't mean that we have to hear the Messiah's footsteps all of the time. In fact, when we do, it can create problems. Harvey Cox, the Harvard theologian, tried to live a version of those footsteps after reading Martin Buber's *I and Thou*. Buber writes about the possibility of realizing the fullness of who we are by treating each encounter with the people we meet as a sacred event. After all, if every person I meet is an image of God, what wouldn't I do for them? How could I pass casually over the opportunity to get to know them better, interact with them fully, and be responsive to their needs? Jesus expressed this recognition of the sacredness of each human life and all human encounters when he said, "That which you do for the least of these, you do for me."

Cox decided to put this insight into practice. This sounds so promising, so inspiring, but it drove people crazy. The guy he bought his paper from in Harvard Square didn't need an I-and-thou encounter; he needed his twenty-five cents! Perhaps when the Messiah comes, every moment will be an encounter with the sacred, but for now, at least, sometimes distance and even casualness has a place. To treat each person as though he or she had infinite value would only be workable given infinite time and resources, which we don't have. The Talmudic story of Hillel is an example of personal sensitivity, not good public policy. Providing that one man with all that he wanted and, in principle, deserved would have denied others any chance of getting even a little bit of the charity to which they were equally entitled. But Buber and Cox and the messianic hope can help us find our way toward richer relationships and a better world by inspiring us to see the potential of each meeting, each encounter, *every* human being.

The search for goodness or God or meaning or the Promised Land or even the Messiah is really about the pursuit. I think that's what my teacher Yitz Greenberg meant when he said the Messiah was the bunny that kept the greyhounds of civilization running. It may be that we will never catch the bunny, but look on the bright side: If we are in search of the unattainable, how can we fail if we're hot on the bunny's heels? Can we give ourselves permission not to get there without being cynical about the journey and maintaining our ability to celebrate all of the achievements along the way? That's what it means to be happy with one's lot, even as we insist that life can always be better, which is a loose translation of how the rabbis defined what it means to be happy in life.

Maimonides, picking up the teaching of ancient rabbis, said that there will be only one difference between this world and the world when the Messiah comes: the Jewish people will no longer be oppressed and will be free to control their own affairs. That insight shouldn't be limited to Jews alone. We could imagine a world when the Messiah comes where no people will be oppressed, where freedom to pursue what we most want will be guaranteed. We must remember, however, that the freedom to pursue what we want most doesn't guarantee a happy outcome for all people. If one nation wants to dominate another, then suffering will continue. If one person needs to take advantage of another in order to feel strong, suffering will continue. If my being right demands that I struggle to ensure that everybody thinks you are wrong, the suffering will continue. The outcomes depend on us. Maimonides imagines a messianic moment in which we have the capacity to realize our dreams, but what we dream, of course, is up to us.

I long to live in a world where there is no violence, sickness, or death. But even in that perfect world, our old set of questions will surely open up new ones. What will it mean to feel rich when we all can have all the material wealth we want? What will it mean to treasure each moment, when we know that we will live forever? What will it mean to enjoy good health when we no longer fear disease? We will finally be free to measure meaning, good fortune, and success against our deepest desires, not our sense that meaning, goodness, and success are scarce commodities. Our tendency is to "count our blessings" in relation to someone else's "curses," or at least their shortcomings. We have a tendency to appreciate what we have in relationship to how little of it someone else has, whether it is material wealth, health, happiness, or anything else, and we treat our blessings like wheat or pork bellies: if the market is full of them, they are worth less, but if they are rare, their value soars.

I want to enjoy my kids' health, as it is, not because there are kids who are suffering more than they are. I want to appreciate my wife, not because of how many people I know who are less happy in their marriages than I am. I want to feel successful without looking down at those people I have "surpassed" along the way. That's when real happiness is found. Being happy with what you have is the real definition of wealth.

When the Messiah comes, our longed-for "there" will become our commonplace "here and now." Our dreams will become our reality, and it will be time to dream new dreams.

Maybe I'm trying to have it all—which only makes me like everyone else I know. That's fine as long as I remember that as soon as I have what I want now, there will be new things to want. I once thought that celebrating my father's eightieth birthday would be "everything," especially since Becky's dad died at sixty (there I am, succumbing to my commodity of joy model again!). Now I want to see his ninetieth, and if we are fortunate enough to make that, I am sure that I will long to see him turn one hundred. As long as we can be happy with what we've got, then wanting more will never be a problem. That's the kind of redemption for which I'm waiting, one that propels me into the future while helping me to enjoy the present.

I actually think it is in us to overcome sickness, hunger, and, yes, as long as we're trying to have it all, death. Maybe that is what Maimonides is saying—that if we took away the barriers in our lives to pursue what we really wanted, if we ended the various types of oppression that are holding back the true potential of our human spirit, then I don't know if we could get all the way to the messianic ideal, but we could get a lot closer than we are now.

Sometimes all you have to do to make barriers go away is to imagine that they're not really there. Even if they are there and you live as though they're not, they tend to disappear.

That is what happened in the Gdansk shipyard uprising in Poland. When it was clear that the uprising wasn't going away, the Russians became involved and sent in tanks. Adam Minchik, Lech Walesa's number two, was asked by a journalist how he could function with tanks parked nearby, pointing their guns at him. "I live as if they weren't there," he replied.

That as-if-ness is an amazing thing. We love our children and our parents as if they haven't disappointed us. We love our spouses as if they haven't hurt and betrayed us. We negotiate treaties as if prior treaties haven't been broken. That's what it means to be idealistic, to be hopeful, to be faithful, to be filled with faith that more is always possible than we first imagined. Of course, if we do that too much, we're fools—but nobody can tell us when we have the mix exactly right, but us.

The story of Dorothy, Toto, and the wizard might help us appreciate the tension between being filled with faith and fooling ourselves about what's possible. If the messianic world we want is an Oz, the place where all questions are finally answered and all of our needs are completely met, then we have to be prepared for a four-foot-nine-inch bald guy who says: pay no attention to the man behind the curtain. I say that as someone who longs for Oz. I don't want to give up on the Emerald City, a place to which we could be traveling, inside of us or an actual locale (hence the double meaning of *lekh lekha*—either go to yourself, or get moving!), where we will find a better self and a better world.

My messianic vision is not about our lives or human history working toward some blissed-out state. It is not about coming to the end of the journey and saying, "Now I can lie down." I hope I'm lucky enough that the journey never ends.

Professor Yishayahu Leibowitz, one of Israel's great public intellectuals and a famous iconoclast, once said, "The only Messiah I can believe in is one who never comes." Leibowitz was reminding us that the things we love most are always in danger of becoming false idols. He would refer to the Western Wall in Jerusalem, the *Kotel* in Hebrew, considered by many to be Judaism's holiest place, as the Discotel, poking fun at the fervent shaking and *shuckling* (a Yiddish word that describes the swaying motion of Jewish prayer) by those who pray there (including me from time to time), and reminding us that nothing is inherently holy. We could just as easily build a discotheque in that location, according to Leibowitz. Places and objects become sacred because of what we invest in them, and it is our investment that is sacred.

When the Bible describes the Ark of the Covenant (you know, what Indiana Jones rescued from the Nazis) and the tabernacle in which the Ark was to be placed, God commands, "Let them make me a place that is made holy, and I will dwell among them." *Mikdash,* the Hebrew word usually translated as "holy place," is actually better rendered as "a place that is made holy." And the passage does not say that God will dwell in that place. It says, "I will dwell among them [i.e., the ancient Israelites]." The implication is that no place can contain what's holy. That holiness, or at least its potential, is everywhere. We simply build places that focus our attention and purpose and in which our sense of the sacred is heightened. That is true for the tabernacle and the Western Wall, as well as for the Kaaba in Mecca. They are all sacred because people have made them sacred. When we make them sacred independent of people, they are nothing more than idols. But that doesn't mean I have a problem with holy places.

I love holy places. They can be taxicabs or an improvised synagogue inside a mosque in Hebron, or the tombs of our forebears or an actual mosque in Plainfield. They can be airport departure lounges or the fields of Canaan, the halls of a hospital or the one remaining wall of the great temple in Jerusalem. All those places can be holy as long as we remember that that sacredness is all around us. They are reminders to us of the sacredness of the entire creation, not places that concentrate sacredness because it's nowhere else.

We all have this ability to tap into the deep spiritual content that the surface of our lives too often obscures.

Friends in Las Vegas recently sent me an e-mail in which they asked me the meaning of the five Hebrew letters that spell the word *emunah,* which means "faith." I sent them back the translation of the word and asked them what was up.

It turned out that James, their twenty-two-year-old musician son, had requested that they turn the word *emunah* into some kind of jewelry that he could wear to remind him not to lose faith in himself, in his music, in who he was.

I explained to his parents that the word not only meant "faith," but was the same word found in the recitation by observant Jews as they bound *tefillin* on their wrists each morning. The verse is "I bind you to me in faith." The language of binding is a double entendre, meaning both a binding of oneself to God and the binding of oneself in marriage. The verse asks, "What am I tied to? What are my commitments?" It takes courage to tie ourselves to anything.

"Your son has connected to the deep wisdom of looking at his body to remind him of what is most deeply in his heart," I told his parents.

His mother was amazed. Coincidentally, the jewelry that they ended up creating for their son was a bracelet of woven black leather straps. "Can you think of any sacred object with black straps?" I asked. "Isn't that what *tefillin* are?" she replied.

"Exactly. That's why this is so moving. The three of you have created a kind of contemporary *tefillin* that helps your son confront the biggest questions in his life by reminding him that he is up to the challenge, and that he will never be alone." His mother started to cry, and I told her how moved I was by what they had done. It was a powerful example of the deep spiritual intuition that we all share. (By the way, the family had an identical bracelet made for me, which I now wear.) I was reminded of Rabbi Kook's words: "I search endlessly for the content of my soul, and external entanglements divert me from this internal search. We all search the four corners of the earth in vain for that which can only be found within the depths of our own souls."

The development of our spiritual intuition reveals the footsteps of the Messiah here and now on earth, not in some future time and other place. The rabbis rarely discuss paradise, the Garden of Eden, in relation to the messianic world. For them the Garden is a synonym for the hereafter. Perhaps they're telling us that our aspirations for his world should be *bigger* than that ancient paradise. In the garden, Adam and Eve could not answer the oldest question in human history: "Where are you?" In fact, it would be twenty generations before Abraham was able to say, "Here I am," as if to answer that question, which had been hanging over the human race for all those years. Only when we are willing to say "Here I am" can the journey really take off. For me, redemption is as simple as the opportunity for each of us to be able to answer that question.

When I was in the yeshiva, each morning we'd put our *tefillin* on before prayer and, using a mirror, check to see whether the *tefillin* were sitting in the precisely prescribed position midway up the forehead and symmetrically between our eyes. At some point in this process, I began to let my gaze move down from the *tefillin* to look into my own eyes before I began to pray in the morning. I think I began to appreciate that until I journeyed inward, I could not journey outward or upward. I began to realize that until I was ready to confront myself, I had no business confronting anyone else—that prayer, whatever else it was, was an exercise in that confrontation with who I was and who I wanted to be.

When I was in Israel recently for my niece's bat mitzvah, my younger brother, who is also a rabbi, shocked me by teaching brilliantly on this theme. His brilliance didn't shock me; I already knew that about him. What shocked me was his willingness to teach this message. Frankly, he's a lot straighter than I am, and we often avoid discussions about our spiritual lives and some of the ideas that I teach, which I know make him uncomfortable. Still, we are very close. My brother Hal, also called by his Hebrew name, Zvi, is one of my best friends. I cannot imagine a triumph not celebrated with him nor a tragedy not shared with him.

The bat mitzvah took place in the Israeli settlement Alon Shvut, where Hal lives with his wife and four children. While far from being a hotbed of radical right-wing politics, it is not a place in which I have many political conversations, either. Geographically halfway between Jerusalem and Hebron, it's not all that far from where my bus was attacked twenty-four years ago. It's ideologically halfway between the two holy cities as well. Being there as I wrote this book was poignant for many reasons.

My dad had just recently had a stroke, and my parents were unable to travel, leaving me as the oldest member of my family in attendance. As I stood in the synagogue, I remembered when my *bubbe* died (soon after she saw me in a yarmulke, though I'm fairly confident that seeing me did not hasten her demise!). I thought about the deaths of my grandparents, and wondered how much longer my parents would be with us.

They were deeply missed, but their physical absence opened up a space for their spiritual presence. It opened up reflective space. I felt the fragility of all our blessings. I treasured my father, standing in the synagogue in Alon Shvut. Why did it take a stroke for me to figure out how to feel the fierce protective love I felt for him? I wanted to live that way moment by moment, with that love always in the forefront of my mind and burning in my heart.

I sat up late one night talking with Hal after everybody had gone to bed. We talked about our parents and how they made us nuts, and about our concerns for their health, and about the inevitable sorrows and challenges of the years ahead. We talked about how they had supported us in becoming who we most wanted to be. They gave us the opportunities to be successful, not in being carbon copies of them, but by becoming genuine versions of ourselves.

That was what my brother taught on the morning of his daughter's bat mitzvah. He said that the only way to find God or the meaning and purpose of your life is to go inside yourself. We are all searching for meaning and purpose, for something larger than ourselves (and it is that search that produces the footsteps of the Messiah). Perhaps, Hal said, that was why the priests bathed their feet in bowls of water before they served in the temple. They would see their reflections in those bowls. I had never told him about how I used mirrors, and I was moved that we had both come to this teaching, each in his own way.

It reminded me of another practice, which I would normally never have shared with him. It would have struck him as a little too unorthodox, but, in light of his own teaching, I decided to.

I've noticed that sometimes when I speak in people's homes there are pictures of Hasidim dancing. "I'm curious," I say to them. "Do you think Hasidim in Brooklyn or Israel have photos of you standing around your Volvo in Scarsdale?"

I think it's great to have pictures of people connecting spiritually in their own way, as long as you have pictures of you doing that, too. I suggest to people that as a personal practice they put those kinds of photos on the wall—along with a mirror. It doesn't matter whether those photos are of lamas in Tibet, shamans in Mexico, or Hasidim in Israel. What's important is that you can see yourself as a spiritual master in the making, ready to be on the wall alongside those other images.

If a mirror on the wall next to the photos is too public, get one of those small mirrors like the ones we used in the yeshiva, and look into your own eyes and ask yourself some simple questions before you get into bed at night or when you wake in the morning. In what ways was I the person I most longed to be today? What helped me to get there? In what ways did I fall short? What do I need in my life in order to do better?

Instead of being a symbol for narcissism or to make a fetish of the body, the mirror becomes a sacred object. If we do this practice long enough and regularly enough, we won't only see ourselves in the mirror. We will see the Messiah coming soon.

BIBLIOGRAPHY

Abdul Rauf, Feisal. *What's Right with Islam*, San Francisco: Harper San Francisco, 2004.

Armstrong, Karen. *A History of God*. New York: Knopf, 2000.

Bauman, Zygmunt. *Life in Fragments*. Oxford: Blackwell, 1995.

Beaudoin, Tom. *Virtual Faith*. San Francisco: Josey-Bass, 1998.

Berlin, Isaiah. *The Proper Study of Mankind*. New York: Farrar, Straus and Giroux, 1998.

Bloom, Harold. *The American Religion*. New York: Simon & Schuster, 1992.

Buber, Martin. *I and Thou*. New York: Free Press, 1971.

Cox, Harvey. *Fire from Heaven*. Menlo Park: Addison-Wesley, 1994.

Csikszentmihalyi, Mihaly. *The Evolving Self.* New York: HarperCollins, 1994.

Dalai Lama. *The Universe in a Single Atom.* New York: Broadway, 2006.

Dawkins, Richard. *The God Delusion.* New York: Houghton Mifflin, 2006.

Eck, Diana L. *A New Religious America.* San Francisco: Harper San Francisco, 2001.

Eck, Diana L. *Encountering God, A Spiritual Journey from Bozeman to Banaras.* Boston: Beacon, 1993.

Eco, Umberto. *The Limits of Interpretation.* Bloomington: University of Indiana, 1994.

Eliade Mircea. *The Sacred & the Profane.* New York: Harcourt Brace Jovanovich, 1959.

Feynman, Richard P. *The Pleasure of Finding Things Out.* Cambridge: Perseus, 1999.

Fish, Stanley. *The Trouble with Principle.* Cambridge: Harvard University, 1999.

Fowler, George. *Dance of a Fallen Monk, A Journey to Spiritual Enlightenment.* New York: Anchor Books, 1996.

Fox, Matthew. *Confessions—The Making of a Post-Denominational Priest.* San Francisco: Harper San Francisco, 1996.

Fox, Matthew. *One River, Many Wells.* New York: Putnam, 2000.

Fromm, Erich. *The Art of Loving.* New York: Harper and Row, 1957.

Giamatti, A. Bartlett. *Take Time for Paradise, Americans and Their Games.* New York: Summit, 1989.

Greeley, Andrew M. *Religion As Poetry.* New Brunswick: Transaction, 1995.

Greenberg, Irving. *The Jewish Way*. New York: Summit Books, 1988.

Hampshire, Stuart. *Justice Is Conflict*. Princeton: Princeton University, 2000.

Heschel, Abraham J. *Man Is Not Alone*. New York: Harper & Row, 1951.

Heschel, Abraham J. *The Insecurity of Freedom*. New York: Farrar, Straus and Giroux, 2007.

Kass, Leon R., M.D. *The Hungry Soul*. New York: Free Press, 1994.

Keating, Thomas. *The Better Part*. New York: Continuum International, 2000.

Kepnes, Steven, Peter Ochs, and Robert Gibbs. *Reasoning After Revelation: Dialogues in Postmodern Jewish Philosophy*. Boulder: Westview Press, 1998.

Kimball, Charles. *When Religion Becomes Evil*. San Francisco: Harper San Francisico, 2002.

Kraemer, David. *The Mind of the Talmud*. New York: Oxford University, 1990.

Kushner, Harold S. *Overcoming Life's Disappointments*. New York: Knopf, 2006.

Levinas, Emmanuel. *Difficult Freedom*. Baltimore: Johns Hopkins University, 1990.

Levinas, Emmanuel. *Nine Talmudic Readings*. Bloomington: Indiana University, 1994.

Maalouf, Amin. *In the Name of Identity, Violence and the Need to Belong*. New York: Arcade, 2001.

Miles, Jack. *God—A Biography*. New York: Knopf, 1995.

Needleman, Jacob. *The American Soul*. New York: Tarcher/Putnam, 2002.

Neusner, Jacob. *There We Sat Down: Talmudic Judaism in the Making.* New York: Ktav, 1978.

Ouaknin, Marc-Alain. *The Burnt Book.* Princeton: Princeton University, 1995.

Paigels, Elaine. *Beyond Belief: The Secret Gospel of Thomas.* New York: Random House, 2003.

Ramadan, Tariq. *In the Footsteps of the Prophet.* New York: Oxford University, 2007.

Sexson, Lynda. *Ordinarily Sacred.* Charlottesville: University of Virginia, 1992.

Smith, Jonathan Z. *Imagining Religion, From Babylon to Jonestown.* Chicago: University of Chicago, 1982.

Smith, Jonathan Z. *To Take Place.* Chicago: University of Chicago, 1987.

Stern, Jessica. *Terror in the Name of God: Why Religious Militants Kill.* New York: HarperCollins, 2003.

Talmud Bavli. Translated by Maurice Simon. London: Soncino Press, 1984.

Tanakh: The Holy Scriptures. New York: Jewish Publication Society, 1985.

Tracy, David. *Blessed Rage for Order.* Chicago: University of Chicago, 1996.

Trilling, Lionel. *Sincerity and Authenticity.* Cambridge: Harvard University, 1971.

Wilbur, Ken. *A Brief History of Everything.* Boston: Shambhala, 1996.

Williams, Bernard. *Truth and Truthfulness.* Princeton: Princeton University, 2002.

Williamson, Marianne. *Imagine.* New York: New American
    Library, 2001.

Wilson, David Sloan. *Darwin's Cathedral: Evolution, Religion, and
    the Nature of Society.* Chicago: University of Chicago, 2002.

Wuthnow, Robert. *After Heaven, Spirituality in America Since the
    1950s.* Berkeley: University of California, 1998.

Wuthnow, Robert. *Sharing the Journey.* New York: Free Press,
    1994.

ACKNOWLEDGMENTS

The key to happiness is gratitude, and the gratitude that I feel as I write these words is so very deep, so it is this section of the book that I am most happy to write. I have been blessed by many things throughout my life, but none more profound than the relationships with family, friends, and teachers without whom *You Don't Have to Be Wrong for Me to Be Right* would never have been written. It is a joy to acknowledge them for helping make this book a reality.

I am deeply grateful to Kenneth Wapner for helping me find and capture my own literary voice. From the moment we met, Kenny's excitement about this project never waned, nor did his vision about how to get us there weaken. He pushed me to explore images and ideas in ways that only one who is your teacher can, while sharing the joy of discovery that comes from the most eager of students. An amazing friend, he even put up with the lousy pizza and worse coffee that we often shared in our work together—a true act of devotion from a gourmet like him!

I want to thank Gail Ross and Howard Yoon, whose roles as my literary agents do not begin to describe their role in either my life or the life of this book. They have consistently provided the grounding that allowed this book to grow, but even more, that has helped me to grow as an author and as a person. They helped me trust the intuition that we can dissolve the barriers between the Jewish teachings in which I am steeped and the human community about which I care. From the first conversation over breakfast in Washington, D.C., when Howard told me why I needed to write this book, to Gail and I sharing life stories at my office in New York, I have benefited from their wonderful encouragement, insight, and friendship with every step taken on the journey toward completing this work.

Harmony Books and the Crown Publishing Group have my deepest appreciation for the way in which they have embraced this book from its very beginnings. Harmony publisher, Shaye Areheart, saw possibilities and potential here from our first encounter. And she did so with warmth and wisdom that have inspired me ever since. Her appreciation of the meeting point between finding deeper spiritual meaning, our ability to create a better world, and the role that books can play in that process is amazing. So, too, is the work of my editor at Harmony, Julia Pastore. Her gentle prodding provided the gift of new energy toward the end of the writing process, and her sharp eye for detail and structure kept this project on track throughout its unfolding. Along with the rest of the team at Harmony, they have been a pleasure to work with.

Mo Hassan and Aasiya Zubair at Bridges TV have provided ongoing support in making our show on their network so successful, and provide a wonderful format in which to continue sharing and generating the ideas and values that shape this book. The same must be said for Chad Wilkinson and Scott Newman, producers of the "Hirschfield and Kula" radio show. They bring smarts, fun, and a genuine appreciation of what this is really all about to our weekly living laboratory, exploring the nexus between what's in the news and what's in our hearts.

I owe more than I can say to my colleagues at CLAL—The National Jewish Center for Learning and Leadership, the uniquely interesting and exciting institution where I am privileged to serve as president. It has provided me with a spiritual and intellectual home that has exceeded my wildest hopes and expectations. Both it and the people there are always with me no matter where in the world I find myself. About no one is that truer than Rabbi Irwin Kula, with whom I share the leadership of the organization. His spiritual and intellectual generosity have made the past twelve years possible and I cannot imagine my work without him, his friendship, his loyalty, or his wisdom. Some people pick you up when you are down; others are good at cheering when you are ahead. Irwin has always done both and that is a gift of inestimable value.

I am deeply appreciative of Donna Rosenthal, the executive vice-chairman of CLAL. A clear-eyed executive with an incredible array of talents and accomplishments that help make CLAL all that it is, she makes it possible for me to focus on teaching, writing, and broadcasting. She is also a forward-looking optimist who believes in our work, and that each day will bring new successes and achievements in everything we do. Without that combination, we could not have come as far as we have.

Thanks to Judy Epstein and Janet R. Kirchheimer, talented professionals who make sure that every aspect of my work is maximized and that everything I do runs as smoothly as possible. Whether it is research for shows, managing logistics, or editing my work, they are the best. As is the faculty of CLAL, including Rabbi Tsvi Blanchard, from whom I have learned much over the past twenty-five years; Rabbi Steve Greenberg, who was in the dining hall that first morning I arrived in Israel; and Dr. Michael Gottsegen, whose friendship and thinking over the past dozen years I have cherished. Thanks also to our administrative team: Meredith Appell, Dale Brown, Judy Epstein, Aliza Kaplan, Theresa Peruzza, Anna Rahklin, and Cynthia Schupf.

CLAL's chairs have all played crucial roles not only in leading the organization that I call home, but in making that home one in which to accomplish my work, and for that I am thankful. To Radine Spier and Charles Bronfman, for encouragement at the beginning of my career and the opportunity to grow. To Barbara Friedman, for having the confidence that I could begin to lead an institution. To Tom Katz, for his intelligence and his unflappability. To Fern Hurst, for her willingness to think big and be courageous. And to our incoming chairman, Larry Gellman, for the depth of his friendship, his love of life, his wonderful sense of humor, and his total commitment to success.

I have had many teachers, but none more profound or influential than CLAL's founder and president emeritus, Rabbi

Irving "Yitz" Greenberg. His influence on this book is significant, and my debt to him for all that he has taught me, beyond repayment. It is my honor to call him Rebbe. Yitz's intellectual courage and theological brilliance have inspired an entire generation, and it was my good fortune to study with him intensively at the beginning of my career. From my first encounter with him in his home, I knew that I would follow the ancient rabbis' advice to make this man my teacher even before he knew he wanted me for a student.

I am also fortunate to have incredible friends without whom neither this book nor many of the best things in my life would actually be. There is Gary Davis, who is both a master teacher and a beloved friend, constantly challenging me to grow even as he always supports me wherever I am. Danny and Robin Greenspun prove that friendship at first sight is possible and that with the passage of time the connection only grows deeper and richer. Al Engelberg, whose guidance is wise, vision is clear, and loyalty profound—there is no combination more dear. Louis Norry and Seth Kaplowitz are brothers who are always there, no matter what and no matter when. Andrew Tisch and Mark Fishman make it so easy, giving much and asking little in return. I thank them all.

Thank you to those friends with whom I have shared so many wonderful conversations in so many interesting places that have stimulated my thinking and with whom I have talked out so many of the ideas in this book. Thanks to Louis Benjamin, the curmudgeon; Jed Bergman, the insightful and generous reader; Andrew Eisenberger, the holy atheist; Michael Goldblum, the artist; Giora Katz-Lichtenstein, the genuine seeker; David

Rosenberg, the mensch; and Johnny Scheiner, the tin man—
each of them adds depth, dimension, and a great deal of fun to
my life.

My in-laws, Al and Paula Madansky, have supported me in
every endeavor in my professional life, up to and including this
book, with the kind of intellectual interest, genuine pride, and
real love that is truly amazing. Perhaps most unusual to be able
to say about one's in-laws, they are wise and loving friends. I
also want to acknowledge Harold Klawans, of blessed memory.
Becky's dad, a grandfather who lit up in the presence of his
grandchildren, a world renowned physician, and an author who
loved to tell stories that translated the wisdom of science into the
lives of regular people. His example was with me throughout the
writing of this book and, though he is missed, he is not gone.

My parents, Joanne and Seymour Hirschfield, have been
my most important role models, and the stories about them in
this book are simply the tip of the iceberg. From them I learned
that passion and commitment can be combined with openness
and inclusiveness. Many people speak of unconditional love, but
they live it. There has never been a moment in my life when that
was in question and that is the greatest gift of all. That, and the
siblings that they gave me: Alan, Linda, and Hal, each of whom
has mastered the art of living full, creative lives marked by
wonderful loving families of their own. Although we are spread
across the world, it is always a joy to be with them and they are
always in my heart.

Finally there is my own immediate family, which is my
heart. We are blessed with three wonderful daughters—Dassi,
Avi, and Dini—each of whom is a gift. I have learned more from

them than they will ever know, at least until they are blessed with children of their own. If theirs are anything like them, then they will join the ranks of the world's luckiest people. Finally, and most dearly, is Becky, for whom there are simply not enough words. She is the one with whom I share everything and who enriches everything I share with her. For over twenty years, she has remained the best thing in my life and a source of boundless energy, unwavering commitment, and profound love that teach me, empower me, and inspire me. Becky is my best friend, the love of my life, and the only one for me. She provides strength, wisdom, and love that nobody could deserve, but for which I am grateful every day.

INDEX

About the Author

Acclaimed speaker, thinker, and commentator on the role of religion, society, and popular culture, RABBI BRAD HIRSCHFIELD is the co-host of the popular weekly radio show "Hirschfield and Kula" on KXL in Portland, Oregon. Creator and host of the multi-part series *Building Bridges: Abrahamic Perspectives on the World Today*, now in its second year airing on Bridges Television (American Muslim TV), he was named one of the Top 50 Rabbis in America in *Newsweek* magazine.

Rabbi Hirschfield is president of CLAL—The National Jewish Center for Learning and Leadership, a national think tank, leadership training institute, and resource center. Recognized as one of the nation's leading Preachers and Teachers by Beliefnet.com, the Web's most popular site for religion, he is a frequent speaker at forums around the country and world. Appearing at the Fes Festival of World Sacred Music and Colloquium in Morocco, and the 2004 Parliament of the World's Religions in Barcelona, where he was featured in the acclaimed film *Freaks Like Me*, as well as at the Aspen Institute, the Washington National Cathedral, many leading universities, and other institutions, he is often quoted by the press. A popular media analyst, he appeared on ABC-TV's *Nightline UpClose* (the only rabbi featured), and PBS-TV's *Frontline: Faith and Doubt at Ground Zero*, is a regular on Court TV, was a commentator for WWSB-TV (ABC affiliate) in Florida, and can often be heard on Public Radio, Westwood One, and many stations nationwide. His op eds have appeared in numerous publications.

Rabbi Hirschfield is the editor of *Remember for Life* (Jewish Publication Society, 2007), and the co-author of *Embracing Life & Facing Death: A Jewish Guide to Palliative Care* (CLAL, 2003). An orthodox rabbi, he is the Scholar-in-Residence for several leading Jewish institutions and is currently working on a new TV series for Bridges Television. He lives in Riverdale, New York, with his wife, Becky, and his three daughters, Dassi, Avi, and Dini.

EXAMINING THE CHALLENGES WE FACE IN LIVING TOGETHER peacefully, respectfully, and joyfully on this small planet, *You Don't Have to Be Wrong for Me to Be Right* is a thoughtful, thought-provoking look at how the things that make us different also make us alike—in both religious and secular life. This reader's group guide is intended as a starting point for your own conversation on these ideas.

READER'S GROUP GUIDE

1. What, if any, religion do you practice? What drew your group to this book? Are you the same religion as the other members of your group? If not, do you have any qualms about discussing religious issues with them? Were your feelings influenced by *You Don't Have to Be Wrong for Me to Be Right*?

2. On page 10, Hirschfield says "ultimately it is the fanaticism that kills, not the faith." Discuss the role of fanaticism in world events—both abroad and here at home.

3. Reinhold Niebuhr said "Fanatic orthodoxy is never rooted in faith but in doubt; it is when we are not sure that we are doubly sure." Do you think this is true? Why might a person who was unsure be more strident in defending his beliefs?

4. Share your favorite passage from *You Don't Have to Be Wrong for Me to Be Right*. What is its message? Why is it meaningful to you?

5. Hirschfield describes faith as "a loving acceptance of the profound complexity of existence and creation. It is about abiding in mystery. In being unsure." How do you define faith?

6. What is the link between spareribs and honoring your mother and father? Discuss how this kind of unlikely connection, in which a seeming contradiction is actually a sacred teaching, could help people of all religions to better understand their own faith and that of their neighbors.

7. What is the difference between a pilgrim, a tourist, and a seeker? Which would you consider yourself? Are you content with that label?

8. Discuss the concepts of victim and victimizer. What danger lies in being a victim? A victimizer? Do you believe that people can be both at the same time?

9. In *You Don't Have to Be Wrong for Me to Be Right*, Hirschfield quotes this passage from *The End of Faith* by Sam Harris: "We must find a way to a time when faith," writes Harris, "without evidence, disgraces anyone who would claim it. Given the present state of the world, there appears to be no other future worth wanting. It is imperative that we begin speaking plainly about the absurdity of most of our religious beliefs." What do you think about this idea? Given that so much of the violence and war in the world is caused by conflicting religious beliefs, should mankind, as a whole, abandon faith? What do you think the result of such an action would be?

10. Discuss the concepts of forgiveness, justice, and vengeance in both personal relationships and interfaith relations. How are they linked and how are they different? Also, consider the role of mercy.

11. In chapter four, Hirschfield discusses the death penalty. What do you think of his ideas on the subject? What do you think of the death penalty in general?

12. Is it important to you that your children marry members of the religion you practice? Why or why not?

13. What do you think about the biblical teachings often called on to support and condemn gay marriage? What is your position on this issue and why? On page 145, Hirschfield calls for both sides of this issue—and other debates facing us in public life today—to admit that they might be wrong and the other side might be right. Do you think that's possible? How would attitude affect public discourse on any subject? Would it be possible to think and act that way and still conduct the business of passing laws to govern the land?

14. Discuss Hirschfield's experience at the Islamic Society of North America. In his position, would you have joined your hosts in prayer

or simply observed from the doorway? Why? Do you believe in the possibility of lasting peace between Jews and Muslims?

15. The following quote appears on page 152: "The more traditionally religious you are, the more deeply modest and radically inclusive you should be. After all, if your tradition truly is the infinite gift of an infinite God, then how could there be only one way to understand it?" Do you agree with this statement? Do you think the teachings of most religions would agree with this statement?

16. In Chapter 7, Hirschfield deals with the concept of the whole being greater than the sum of its parts by describing his experience at a ceremony to mark the reopening of a synagogue outside of the Polish town Oswiecim, called Auschwitz by the Nazis. How does his visit to a Catholic mass held in celebration of the reopening both surprise him and reconfirm his ideas about how we can best live together peacefully? What does the Bishop Ricoczy represent to the Rabbi?

17. On pages 199–200, Hirschfield writes: "If all I am is that which you are not, then I have given over control of my identity to you! It is precisely when I can connect to you while maintaining my personal integrity that I find out who I most deeply am." What does this statement mean to you?

18. Do you think that saying both sides of the abortion debate "believe in the sanctity of life and the dignity of human beings" (page 202) oversimplifies the issue? Do you agree with the idea that both pro-life and pro-choice activists care about the same thing—although one group is focused on the mother and one on the unborn child?

19. Hirschfield translates the Hebrew word *ezer k'negdo,* used in Genesis to describe Eve as "a helper who is *against him.*" Does this make sense to you? How can someone help you and be against you at the same time? Is it possible to disagree with someone on life's big issues and still connect with them?

20. In personal and political life, why is it important to engage those whose beliefs are the furthest removed from your own in conversation? Hirschfield declines an invitation to join a breakfast hosted by

Iranian president Ahmadinejad. Why? In Hirschfield's shoes, would you have attended?

21. On page 219, Hirschfield offers an interesting take on the motivating forces behind fanaticism and zealotry. What do you think of his idea?

22. Discuss the seven steps Hirschfield lays out to help us talk to one another in a way that guarantees that we put "the dignity of the person in front of us before the correctness of our own ideas." The story begins on page 216.

23. What's the difference between naïveté and idealism? Do you think Hirschfield is naïve? Idealistic? Correct? Would it be possible to live as he proposes?

24. Discuss the version of the coming—or return—of the Messiah found on page 239: "We could imagine a world when the Messiah comes where no people will be oppressed, where freedom to pursue what we most want will be guaranteed. We must remember, however, that the freedom to pursue what we want most doesn't guarantee a happy outcome for all people. If one nation wants to dominate another, then suffering will continue. If one person needs to take advantage of another in order to feel strong, suffering will continue. If my being right demands that I struggle to ensure that everybody thinks you are wrong, the suffering will continue. The outcomes depend on us."